# A Sassy Guide to Cronehood

Finally, a book on the true nature of menopause: celebration! This book confirms what you've always suspected: that personal value, self-worth, and beauty all increase with age. You'll jump eagerly into maturity, which is, after all, the true beginning of life's liberties and freedom. Finally, you'll revel in the discovery that youth is only a dress rehearsal for the fun, happiness, and satisfaction that come with the menopausal transition.

*In Praise of the Crone* explores the physical and spiritual issues that you'll face in your journey through menopause, providing practical advice and solutions to menopausal concerns along the way. Spells, formulas, rituals, recipes, charts, and meditations on the issues surrounding menopause are enhanced by an informative appendix of herbs, flowers, stones, and female deities.

Take this opportunity to introduce yourself to your personal Crone. Welcome your spirit self back into your life. Gather up your sass, kick that pesky self-doubt to the curb, and let's get this party started!

# About the Author

Dorothy Morrison lives the magical life in the boot heel of Missouri with her husband and teenage son. They share their home with two feisty Labrador Retrievers, Sadie Mae and Jonah, various tropical fish, and a large assortment of African violets. She is a Wiccan High Priestess of the Georgian Tradition and founded the Coven of the Crystal Garden in 1986. An avid practitioner of the Ancient Arts for more than twenty years, she teaches the Craft to students throughout the United States and Australia. She is also a member of the Pagan Poet's Society.

An archer and bow hunter, Dorothy regularly competes in outdoor tournaments and holds titles in several states. Her other interests include Tarot work, magical herbalism, and stonework, as well as computer networking with those of like mind.

# To Write to the Author

If you would like to contact the author or would like more information about this book, please write to the author in care of Llewellyn Worldwide and we will forward your request. Both the author and the publisher appreciate hearing from you and learning of your enjoyment of this book and how it has helped you. Llewellyn Worldwide cannot guarantee that every letter written to the author can be answered, but all will be forwarded. Please write to:

Dorothy Morrison
c/o Llewellyn Worldwide
P.O. Box 64383, Dept. K468-5
St. Paul, MN 55164-0383
U.S.A.

Please enclose a self-addressed, stamped envelope for reply or $1.00 to cover costs. If outside the U.S.A., please enclose an international postal reply coupon.

A Celebration of
Feminine Maturity

# In Praise
## of the
## Crone

## Dorothy Morrison

1999
Llewellyn Publications
Saint Paul, Minnesota 55164-0383
U.S.A.

FIRST EDITION
First Printing, 1999

Cover Design: Anne Marie Garrison
Interior Design and Editing: Kjersti A. Monson
Interior Illustrations: Lauren Foster-MacLeod

**Library of Congress Cataloging-in-Publication Data**
Morrison, Dorothy, 1955–
    In praise of the crone : a celebration of feminine maturity
Dorothy Morrison. – 1st ed.
      p.  cm.
    Includes bibliographical references and index.
    ISBN 1-56718-468-5 (trade paper)
    1. Witchcraft.   2. Menopause–Miscellaneous.   I. Title.
BF1572.M46M67   1999
133.4'3–dc21                                 98-42216
                                                        CIP

The remedies in this book are not meant to diagnose, treat, prescribe, or substitute consultation with a licensed healthcare professional. Furthermore, the recipes herein are not intended for commercial use or profit.

Llewellyn Publications
A Division of Llewellyn Worldwide, Ltd.
P.O. Box 64383, Dept. K468-5
St. Paul, MN 55164-0383

Printed in the United States of America

# Other Books by Dorothy Morrison

*Magical Needlework*
Llewellyn Publications, 1998

*Everyday Magic*
Llewellyn Publications, 1998

*The Whimsical Tarot*
Deck and book; U.S. Games Systems Inc., 1998-99

*To my mother, my grandmother,*
*my aunts, and to the tens of*
*thousands of other women who*
*made this transition without*
*help, without support, and*
*without ever finding one single,*
*solitary reason to celebrate.*

# The Crone

By the fire, She sits, the Crone
Relaxing there upon Her throne
Of vines that intertwine and twirl
Within the foggy, misty swirl
The twinkling eyes that light the dark
The smile that warms the night so stark
Belie Her sassy disposition
A pure and simple contradiction
To everything that you've been told
About the Crone, so wise and old
Her laughter rings out through the night
She claps Her hands in pure delight
At the joke She's helped to play
On those afraid to pass Her way
For She knows She's nothing like
The Wretch of whom historians write
Instead, She's hip and full of fun
And rewards you for a job well done
By offering Her many treasures
Her friendship, love, and joyful pleasures
The only catch, please understand
Is that you have to take Her hand

—*Dorothy Morrison*

# Contents

# Acknowledgments

My mother always said that the hug was the most important gesture ever invented. She was right. That one little movement can say more in a split second than any lengthy soliloquy ever could. It says "I love you," "I couldn't have done it without you," and "You're important." Sometimes, it even says "I'm just glad you're you." No matter what the message, it usually conveys that the person on the receiving end is somehow responsible for a joyous feeling, a lightened heart, and a reason to celebrate.

Though many people worked hard to put this book on the shelves and are to be congratulated, some went above and beyond all expectation to make its manifestation a celebratory event. While I'd like to give each and every one of them a great big hug, it's just not possible to do that on paper. Instead, I'll have to do the next best thing and use a phrase to convey my sentiments. It's nearly as short, nearly as celebratory, and just as simple. The phrase, of course, is thank you!

To She-Who-Nags, Who entered my life with such brash force that I never thought I'd have a nice thing to say about Her. I was wrong. With no regard for my reluctance, She became my friend, my mentor, and my confidante. She helped me when no one else could, and loved me no matter what I did. Most importantly, She allowed me to share Her celebratory wisdom with the world.

To the incredible women of my ancestry who unknowingly gave me an unsurpassed personal heritage, and whose bloodlines and collective consciousness lives on within me.

To my husband, Spook, whose love for me never faltered, even when I tested his patience!

To Gay, who listened to my rantings, restored my confidence on a regular basis, and was always there when I needed her.

To InaRae, whose constant letters of encouragement always made me smile, and whose special kind of camaraderie shaped the tone of this book.

To Carol Dow, whose delightful comments continually lifted my spirits and kept me going when I didn't think I could.

To Sandra and Carl Weschcke, and all the other folks at Llewellyn, who believed in this book and allowed me to introduce She-Who-Nags to the world.

Most especially though, to you, the reader. By opening this book, you've taken the challenge of reinventing your life, and restructuring your strand in the Cosmic Web. This journey is special, and you'll need courage, conviction, and tenacity to see it through. There may be a pitfall or two along the way. But at the end of it all, you'll have what you need. It's a sense of belonging, a sense of understanding, a sense of feeling complete. You'll have something that most folks search a lifetime for but never find: a real reason to celebrate!

# Preface

Menopause. I have to admit that I'd never really thought of it as being a passage into spiritual wisdom, or anything more than a royal pain in the butt, until recently. How could I? How could anyone else, for that matter? The very sound of the word conjures up thoughts of hormone imbalance, hot flashes, night sweats, and unreasonable, opinionated women just waiting for a chance to throw the next temper tantrum. Chaotic and discordant? Maybe. Spiritual? Hardly!

My mother had an awful time with menopause. I was conceived at about the time her body started to change, and the pregnancy wasn't an easy one. Even worse, I was a very large baby, and (much to her dismay) I turned out to be the most active of her children. My birth resulted in an awful bout of postnatal depression. Mama didn't know anything about herbal treatments, and estrogen therapy hadn't yet been invented. Sadly enough, she lived the next twenty years or so in misery. That period of her life is marked indelibly on my brain and, as a Christian child, I remember thinking how cruel God was to hate women so much.

Seeing things from that point of view, it's little wonder that I had a good laugh when, during my early Pagan days, I walked in on a discussion regarding the virtues of menopause. There they were: a group of female elders talking about its spiritual wonders and the many joys it brought to their lives. Well, I thought, that just proved they'd lost their minds as well as their menses! I remarked that there was nothing joyous about night sweats, and certainly nothing wondrous about the depression that often accompanies that particular transition. I went on to say that I hoped the Lady would see fit to remove me to the Summerland before it happened to me. That final note of disrespect was met by a chorus of silvery laughter. It was the laughter of experience—the laughter that comes from living, doing, and knowing, rather than from only imagining.

No smart-alecky remark has ever rolled off my tongue that didn't come back to haunt me, and this case was no exception. The Lady, in Her infinite wisdom, did not remove me from the planet before menopause. Instead, She saw to it that I carefully aligned myself with the deities who could help me most, then hurled me irrevocably into the menopausal pit at the early age of thirty-two.

At first, the changes in my body terrified me; I'd already experienced their horrors with my mother. The hot flashes that came in the dead of winter were more than a little embarrassing. The night sweats hit and I developed a severe case of insomnia. Sex wasn't as much fun and, to top it off, depression reared its ugly head and ate me for lunch. For the first time in my life, I had no energy. I was a listless, lethargic mess. I was miserable.

There I sat, day in and day out, firmly planted on my pity pot. How did other women cope with this awful mess? And then I heard it. A single word.

"Celebrate." It was my spirit guide.

"What?!" Surely I hadn't heard him correctly!

"Celebrate." The second response was as flat as the first.

Now I wasn't just miserable, I was indignant!

"Really?! What could *you* possibly know about the change of life? You're not even a woman!"

"Celebrate." Then he was gone.

For a while I grumbled over the absurdity of his statement. Then I ranted and raved that the Lady was just as uncaring as the Christian God. After all, She'd given me a male spirit guide who had no idea how to help me. I screamed. I yelled. I tossed things across the room. I threw the nastiest hissy fit in the history of womankind. Then I sat down to think.

Celebrate. I rolled the word over and over in my head. Finally, I said the word out loud. Even its sound had a joyous ring. I saw the images it evoked and thought about all of the reasons for celebration. Two words encompassed them all: special events. Okay, I reasoned, maybe my initial perspective was way off. I still didn't think that menopause was particularly special, and celebrating it seemed a bit ridiculous, but what could it hurt? Worst case scenario? My students would think I'd gone temporarily insane. No problem. They'd thought that before.

Throwing myself into the celebration mode wasn't easy, but I started that very day. I began to pamper myself. I took time out to do things that made me feel good, and tended to my own needs for a change. It seemed a little selfish at first but, before long, I was a much happier person and so were the people around me. I felt special and so did they.

So what does any of this have to do with wisdom and spirituality? Everything! For starters, I realized that my spirit guide wasn't a complete idiot, and that the Goddess hadn't sent him just to annoy me.

Simple as it sounds, that realization opened the door to a world of spiritual enlightenment that I never thought possible. The mysteries unfolded and, for the very first time, the wisdom of their lessons was flawless. My life filled with the synchronicity of the cosmos, and every day I became more acutely aware of its presence in every drop of rain, every step traveled, and every web woven. I heard the Lady in every word spoken and felt Her in each new opportunity that entered my life. Most important, though, I realized that I was the Goddess come full circle . . . a gift much more valuable than youth.

The point is, time spent mourning your lost youth is a waste. Menopause is not some dreaded disease, and its physical symptoms can be eased to near nonexistence. It is not a punishment and shouldn't be regarded as an affliction. It is to be commemorated and cherished like a birthday, a first menses, or a handfasting, for with it come the most precious gifts the Lady has to offer: enlightenment, fresh perspective, and spiritual completion.

That's plenty of reason to celebrate!

# Chapter 1

# Who Are You and What Do You Want with Me?

A few months before I plunged into adult life, a great song hit the charts. I loved the music, loved the beat, and loved the passion in the singer's voice. It wasn't long before I knew all the words and was singing along. But one day, I was struck by the full impact of the song. Instead of only mimicking the singer, I finally paid attention to the message being sent. It was that women were strong people with opinions and ideas. They didn't have to live the life someone else laid out for them. They could claim any life they chose and accomplish anything they wanted. Sometimes, though, they had difficulty being heard. And when that happened, they had to raise their voices. Sometimes they even had to roar.

For me, the song heralded the age of a new kind of woman. I was determined to be one, so roar I did. I zipped through life with the zest of a gazelle, handled a schedule heftier than the president's, and managed a daily juggling act that rivaled David Copperfield's. There wasn't any job too difficult to tackle or any goal I couldn't reach. With so much on my plate, it was a blessing I even remembered my own name. But I did. I had to. I was Woman.

Like other modern women, I was the picture of strength and courage. I was educated, intelligent, and independent. But a single word, *menopause*, claimed a power over me that I couldn't explain. The very sound of it made me feel nauseated. To be perfectly honest, it scared the hell out of me. But I didn't tell anyone. I couldn't. After all, I was Woman.

I had lots of excuses for my fear. I didn't want to deal with night sweats, hot flashes, and anxiety attacks. I worried about exhaustion, mood swings, and personality changes. I was concerned with the sex aspect, too. I'd heard that menopause brought an end to sexual fun and that, no matter how hard you tried, there was no way to retrieve your original passion. When asked how I felt about the transition, though, I never voiced my real fear. I only said that it was the first step toward the end of femininity. Of course, that was a lie.

The real reason for my fear (the one I refused to talk about) was that it brought me face to face with my own personal mortality. Just thinking about it made me feel old, and I didn't like it. I didn't want to be used up, worn out, and worthless. I was important. I had things to say. I needed to be heard, and I knew menopause would steal that from me. No one would listen if I were old. They'd just assume my words were the rantings of senility.

Thankfully, passing years brought me wisdom and a fresh perspective. It finally occurred to me that my initial fears about menopause were not my fault. I hadn't invented them. They'd been strategically placed along my path and, much like a common parasite, they had fed on me until they overtook all common sense. The parasite-placing culprit, of course, was the Analyst—the societal manipulator who lives within all of us.

The Analyst is your worst enemy, and She makes up the whole of societal thinking. She tells you you're not good enough, smart enough, or attractive enough to make it in this world. She stills your tongue when you know you should speak up. She keeps you from reaching your potential by talking you into settling for something less than you deserve. She discounts your ideas as foolishness and squelches your creative force. Her job is to make you feel completely worthless, and she relishes her work.

Now the Analyst is no one's fool, and She pulls out all the stops when it comes to menopause. She waits until our bodies change, our hormones get out of whack, and our emotional power supply reaches rock bottom. Then She steals into our subconscious minds and quietly picks away at what little strength we have left. Suddenly, we feel stupid for asking questions, less than human for saying no, and prehistoric for having values. And that's just the beginning. With the preliminaries out of the way, the Analyst really gets down and dirty. She breathes life into new monstrosities. Self-doubt. Anxiety. Fear. Before we know it, we're reduced to quivering heaps of flesh looking only for a place to hide.

So, is there any way to fight the Analyst? More to the point, can we beat Her at Her own game? You bet. All we have to do is invoke the Crone. She's a tough, formidable adversary and quite capable of stealing the Analyst's thunder. Enlisting Her aid, though, isn't always an easy task. First, you have to befriend Her. And, in my case, that wasn't quite as simple as it sounds.

# She-Who-Nags

It might have been easier for me if our first meeting had been the kind that encouraged friendship. There's usually a "how do you do." A handshake. Maybe even a hug. She-Who-Nags, however, dispensed with all of those niceties. In our first meeting, there wasn't even so much as a "glad to meet you." It was an in-your-face fiasco that began over a tiny plot of weeds.

I was in the garden welcoming newcomers: those sprouts who, just the night before, lay sleeping in the Mother's womb. A goddess chant rolling off my tongue, I encouraged others to push their way through to my world. A pale green blanket covered the garden. The heady scent of sweet peas perfumed the air. Spring had arrived and everything around me was fresh with new life.

So was I. My step was livelier. I was more energetic. I wanted to dance; I wanted to skip; I wanted to run around the block with the joy of being alive. Then I did! Afterward, I laughed out loud at the thought of the neighbors who'd just had the pleasure of watching me (the conservative woman who lived on the corner) make a real spectacle of myself. I'd never felt so young or so vibrant. I was as happy as a hummingbird flitting about in a hibiscus bed.

Then I saw it.

It wasn't very big. It didn't look dangerous. It was green, like the newcomers, and might have been considered pretty if viewed from the right angle. Standing back from the garden, I adjusted my gaze and hoped it would disappear into the sea of new sprouts. It didn't. The fact is, it stuck out like a sore thumb.

"Pull it!" The voice was ancient, but not mild. It sounded like the crackle of lightning in a thunderstorm. I looked around to see who owned the voice. No one came into view. I decided that I was imagining things and started walking toward the back door.

"Hey! Are you deaf? I said, pull it!"

I nearly jumped out of my skin. Who the hell was that and what did She want with me? I didn't turn around. I didn't have to. I knew the voice didn't belong to a body. Goddess! Had I suddenly contracted multiple personality disorder? Determined not to show fear, I took a deep breath and squared my shoulders.

"I beg your pardon?!" The words flew off my tongue with the icy indignation of an old maid school teacher.

"The weed, damn it! Pull the damned weed!"

A sigh of relief swept through my body. I wasn't hearing things. I didn't have to worry about schizophrenia or MPD. Though I'd never heard the voice, I knew the attitude. It belonged to She-Who-Nags, my personal Crone.

For years She'd been pushing me to make the transition into the Crone phase. I didn't want to, and I had a whole lot of excuses to offer as proof of why I shouldn't. First, I explained to Her that I was an Earth Goddess. As such a bountiful, fruitful, and motherly creature, I was obviously just the opposite of everything that She thought I should be. I then mimicked the Analyst, saying that I wasn't old enough, good enough, or wise enough for Cronehood. My words fell on deaf ears. In sheer desperation, I stomped my foot and screamed at the top of my lungs for Her to go away. Finally, I simply went on about the business of ignoring Her.

Obviously, it hadn't worked. Hell bent on teaching me the mysteries and wisdom of the "destructive phase" (I'll explain this shortly), She'd gone to new lengths. She'd sent me out to the garden to pull weeds! I was furious, and I didn't care one bit if She knew it. I spat and sputtered and threw a temper tantrum to rival any respectable five-year-old's.

"What the hell is wrong with You? You know me. I'm the one who has trouble using the fly swatter. And now You expect me to murder that weed?! Surely it's good for something, or the Lady wouldn't have created it. I'll not do it. And You can't make me!"

When She persisted, I marched right into the house and slammed the door. I listened for the crackling voice, but all I heard was silence. The sound was sweet. Peaceful. It settled in all around me. I poured a cup of coffee and giggled at my victory. I'd won and there was nothing She could do about it.

Silly me! She-Who-Nags had hushed, but only long enough to regroup and rework Her strategy. It only took Her a matter of hours. And this time, She used the telephone.

The call in question involved a couple of prestigious game outfitters and an invitation for the bow hunting expedition of a lifetime. Apparently, the feature article I'd written for them had brought in a ton of money, and they wanted to do something nice for me. They'd never had a female archer on the premises and thought it would be excellent for business, regardless of the fact that I hadn't actually gone out and hunted since childhood. Before I could say no, the hunt was set. I had two weeks to get ready.

I wasn't just nervous, I was sick. They were talking about a live animal. My first shot had to count, because I wouldn't have a chance for a second, more perfect arrow placement. Two bottles of Mylanta later, I decided to cancel. After all, I was a grown person, and no one could make me hunt.

Or so I thought.

Before I could cancel, the phone rang. It was the outfitter again, and the stakes had been raised. Now he wanted me to hunt in an area that held only trophy class animals. I tried to interrupt, but he just wouldn't listen. He jabbered right on about record books, publicity, and hunting videos. And before I could get a word in edgewise, he hung up. I looked at the phone in my hand, and heard a gleeful cackle rising above the dial tone.

I was fit to be tied. Whether it was pulling a weed or hunting wild game, I was going to learn my place in the cycle of life and death, of creation and destruction. She-Who-Nags had won.

On the first day of the hunt, I was out for ten hours and never got a shot. Was it possible that She-Who-Nags had sent me on a wild goose chase? Or maybe just given up and gone away? Could I be so lucky? Not a chance. She was simply wearing me down.

The next day brought clear skies with a twist: a ground fog that seemed to rise from the bowels of the Earth covered the land as far as the eye could see. I watched the mist swirl around the field of dead grasses. This was it, I thought. It was a Croney kind of day. I took a deep breath, gathered my wits, and headed for the woods. My shot came less than thirty minutes later. The delivery was flawless and the arrow placement was perfect.

I exhaled fully and began to relax. It was hard to believe I'd been so worried. Bow hunting wasn't difficult. Like everything else in life, it was all a matter of focused perspective.

Finally, I got the point: the creative process, or the life force, blossoms only from *destruction*—the destructive phase. I had to learn this lesson with the literal death and rebirth of physical nutrition found in the food chain. But in all cases, one must sacrifice original form (thereby implying its metaphoric or literal death) in order to witness the rebirth of something new and different.

For the first time in a long while, I felt good about myself. That gnawing feeling in the pit of my stomach was gone. I'd conquered my fear and I had She-Who-Nags to thank.

I laughed out loud at the reality check in progress. My oh my! I realized that there is more to She-Who-Nags than the crusty, stubborn old biddy who delights in making my life miserable. Much more. She has a soft side, too. In the deepest part of Her matrix is a tender, loving Goddess who brings guidance to the confused, power to the helpless, and peace to the overwrought.

Her methodology in this case left something to be desired but, in light of my recent behavior, She had little choice. A sweet, gentle, grandmotherly type could never have helped me. I just wouldn't have listened. As a result, I'd forced She-Who-Nags to rethink Her strategy. She'd become tough. Resourceful. Amazingly creative. She'd smacked me around with a cosmic two-by-four until She got some results. And, as much as I hated to admit it, I found myself growing fond of Her.

# The Personal Crone:
# Who She Is and Who She Isn't

Why is it so hard to befriend the Crone? Maybe it's because She's the most maligned Goddess-form in existence. Mention Her name and what springs to mind? Keeper of the Karmic Keys. Mistress of Darkness. Bringer of Death. At the very least, the mind's eye conjures up visions of a powerful, unyielding, fearsome Goddess. That's not so bad. Our real troubles begin with the misconception that the Crone has a mean streak. Somewhere along the line, we got the idea that She loves to place us in impossible situations, delights in our screw-ups, and lives to dole out hefty doses of Karmic retribution.

It gets worse. We often picture Her as the stereotypical witch. We cover Her in wrinkles, knock out a few teeth and, just for good measure, toss in a wart or two. Before we know it, we've created an archetypical monster—a visage so awful that a single glance would make Medusa faint. It's no wonder we're scared of Her.

Our faulty visions of the Crone terrify Her, too. Even worse, they hurt Her feelings. Try to see it from the Crone's point of view. How would you feel if folks decided, without the benefit of a single conversation, that you were a mean, hateful person? Or, without so much as a single glimpse, insisted that you were too ugly to be looked upon? And then added insult to injury by sharing that newfound "knowledge" with everyone they met? You'd probably think they were a bunch of unfair, narrow-minded jerks with few manners and little common sense. It's highly unlikely you'd even bother to spit on them if they were dying of thirst in the desert, much less jump at the chance to be their friend.

Just for a moment, let's put our imaginations to rest and look at the facts. The Crone is the Keeper of Justice. She is concerned with fairness, with right and wrong. When others wish us ill, treat us poorly, or just refuse to give us a fair shake, it's the Crone Who deals with the mess and fixes the problem. She tosses the obstacles out of our way and helps us get back on track. She is a powerful ally, and we couldn't get through life without Her.

The Crone is, however, a very focused Goddess. She sees things only in black and white, and doesn't give a hoot about extenuating circumstances. Gray areas simply don't exist for Her. She rights every wrong that comes Her way with expedient efficiency. This doesn't mean She's a vindictive or hateful Goddess. It does mean that you need to take a good hard look at any situation before you ask Her for assistance. If you contributed in any way to the mess at hand, She'll make you accountable. Justice is her forté. And when calling on the Crone, justice is exactly what you'll get.

The Crone's title, Bringer of Death, also puts some of us off. That's because we're conditioned to think of death as an end rather than a change of venue or atmosphere. Maybe if we understood the life and death transitions more fully, we wouldn't feel that way. Life is a little like reading a chapter from your favorite book. We follow the story's twists and turns, cheer for the hero, and hiss at the villain. All in all, it's an enjoyable, exhilarating experience. Then we finish the chapter. There's nothing terrifying about that. Excitement mounting, we hurriedly turn the page to see what the next chapter holds. Death is much like the pause between the end of one chapter and the beginning of the next. No other transition fills the spirit with more excitement or anticipation. Undoubtedly, it's the most pleasurable spot in life, and we have the Crone to thank for it.

Perhaps the biggest problem we have with the Crone has to do with our misconceptions of Her appearance. True, She's ancient. But how do we know She has more wrinkles than a Sharpei pup, is missing teeth, or even worse, has warts? The fact is, we don't. Many of us haven't even seen the Crone. The problem is that we judge Her as if She were human, and She's not. She's a Goddess. A shape-shifter. If She desires to, She can look like anyone or anything at all.

Take She-Who-Nags, for instance. She's a hip, wisecracking, silver-haired beauty of about sixty. Her mouth and eyes are faintly lined from laughter. Other than that, there's not a wrinkle in sight. Her face is wartless, Her teeth are all there and, when She smiles, Her eyes sparkle like moonbeams. She's active and sassy, vital and sexy, and has an inner radiance that closely resembles sunshine. Her physical appearance is anything but scary. It's safe to say that your personal Crone won't terrify you either—at least, not with Her appearance!

The Crone is multifaceted and has many aspects seldom noticed by those who don't count Her among their intimate friends. For example, most of us know that She's the Keeper of Wisdom and the Mistress of Sorcery. But it might surprise you to know that She's also the Mistress of Healing. That's not all. She's a freedom-giver. A party animal. The Supreme Humorist. Even better, She's the most trusted confidante you'll ever have. No matter where you've been or what you've done, the Crone understands your most intimate worries, hopes, and dreams. Why? Because the Crone is the total Goddess. She's been there as the Maiden. Done that as the Mother. And on occasion, if you watch very carefully, you may even catch a glimpse of Her wearing the T-shirts as proof of Her experience.

Though all personal Crones share the characteristics mentioned above, none are exactly like She-Who-Nags. They come in as many shapes, sizes, appearances, and personalities as the women they belong to. Yours may be the academic type, the grandmotherly type, or the sincerely spiritual type. Your personal Crone may be sweet and tender, logical and to-the-point, or witty, gregarious, and jovial. One thing's for sure, though. She'll be exactly the type suited to you and your life's lessons. She has to be. Whether you like it or not, your personal Crone is an extension of you.

Your Crone has been with you forever, since the day your spirit was just a thought. She's personally carried you out of your previous lives and led you into every new one. She's supervised your growth experiences, protected you from harm, and carefully placed you on the road to life's lessons. Your every success is Her joy and your every tear, Her sorrow. She's loved you with a love greater than the Mother's and, no matter what, She's never left your side. After all She's done, it's little wonder that the personal Crone gets an attitude now and then, especially when the usual response to Her guidance is fear, disregard, or willful defiance.

For this reason, I urge you not to ignore your Crone. It's the quickest way I know to complicate an otherwise peaceful life. Make the first move. Welcome Her with open arms and embrace Her fully. Better yet, try the ritual below. It will please Her immensely, and save you lots of aggravation in the long run.

## ❖ Personal Crone Welcoming Ritual

**Materials:**

- Purple candle
- Peppermint tea or candy
- Sage Salvia
- 1 piece of black ribbon or cord, the same length as your body
- Raven feather (if not available, any black feather will do)
- Censor or fireproof dish filled with sand

Gather the materials and go to a place where you won't be disturbed. Place the sage in the censor and light it. Light the candle. With each lighting, say:

**I light the fires of wisdom**
**I invite you in, my Crone**

Hold the feather in your dominant hand. Using it as a wand and, traveling deosil (clockwise), cast a triple Circle. On the first pass, say:

> **Crone of Wisdom, Crone of Power**
> **I call You down from Karma's Tower**

On the second:

> **Crone of Power, Crone of Strength**
> **Be my guest and stay at length**

And on the third:

> **Crone of Strength, Omnipotent One**
> **Enter now! So be it done!**

Sit in the center of the Circle. Open your arms in embrace and say:

> **I welcome You, Crone, with wide open arms**
> **My watcher, my teacher, my protector from harm**
> **I offer my friendship and bid you come in**
> **Share my hopes and my dreams**
> **Share my life 'til its end**
> **I offer my love and a friendly fresh start**
> **I open to You both my life and my heart**

Knot the feather in the center of the cord. Tie the cord around your waist and say:

> **I join this symbol of your wisdom**
> **Forever with my measure**
> **I am whole for we are one**
> **I accept You, Crone, with pleasure**

Lift the tea or the candy skyward and say:

> **Bless this bit of ice and fire**
> **With Your wisdom, joy, and laughter**
> **Help rekindle my spiritual fires**
> **And guide me ever after**

Sit comfortably in the center of the Circle and consume the peppermint. Listen carefully, for the Crone may speak to you during this time. You should closely watch your surroundings for changes, too. Her messages don't always come in word form. Sometimes, She works in symbols, signs, and sounds. For example, there may be an unexpected gust of wind, a falling leaf, or a sudden parting of clouds. Remember, even if you don't see or hear anything, it doesn't mean that She's not there. Speak to Her directly. Ask Her questions (Her name is a good starting point) and wait for Her answers. They will come. Talk to her as a friend, and you'll be surprised at how quickly She responds. In fact, once you get Her going, you may never have the luxury of peace and quiet again!

When you feel that the visit has ended, close the Circle by traveling widdershins (counterclockwise) from the east.

As you do, say:

**We close this sacred Circle now**
**My Crone and I together**
**We are joined from this day on**
**By bond of cord and feather**

Take the cord from your waist and keep it in a safe place. It's an important magical tool now (a link to your Crone) and can be used for calling Her anytime you like.

# Rebirthing the Spirit Self

She-Who-Nags and I have come a long way since our rocky beginnings, and over the years we've developed quite a relationship. I've discovered that She has a great sense of humor as well as a love of the ridiculous. We laugh. We share. We have fun. My staunchest defender,

She holds my hand when I'm afraid and kicks me in the butt when I need it. She boosts my confidence and delights in my success. She's my best friend.

Our friendship didn't happen overnight, though. It took a lot of work on my part. I hadn't been the easiest person to get along with, and Her feelings were hurt. There was more to it than a simple apology. I had to get to know Her—get under Her skin and figure out what made Her tick. To do that, of course, I had to rediscover myself. And that meant rediscovering the Crone twin.

Most folks don't realize that the Crone has a twin. Well, She does. The Crone twin is the spiritual part of you, your link to the Crone's wisdom, and the person you were born to be. Vibrant. Empowered. Unique. At least, she was. That was before society and the Analyst squelched her beneath their thumbs, robbed her of power, and turned her into a manageable clone.

Expedient revival of the Crone twin (sometimes known as the Spirit Self) is not only *important* during menopause, it's imperative. Why? Because the twin brings balance, stability, and focus to our lives. She helps us see the changes in our bodies for what they are: freedom from the responsibilities of puberty and motherhood, and the opportunity to experience life anew.

Aside from that, the Crone twin's absence from our lives is what gives the Analyst power and keeps the personal Crone from getting through. This is the very thing that stops us from listening to our inner voice and heeding its advice. Our positive energy flow, physical vitality, and the natural healing capacities of the mind and body are impeded. Even worse, the connection between our physical and spiritual worlds is blocked. Once that happens, the creative flow wanes and any personal magical power begins to stagnate. Believe me, it isn't a pretty picture.

Fortunately, the Crone twin isn't lost forever. It's possible to track her down, give her new life, and renew her strength and courage. All it takes is a little time, minimal effort and, of course, the exercises in this book. As you do them, your Crone and Her twin can easily merge again and bring you the most precious gifts life has to offer: feminine wisdom, power, and magic.

## ❖ The Rebirthing Ritual

This is an eight-day ritual. Although it can be performed at any time except the Waning Moon, it's most effective when begun one week before the Full Moon.

### Day One

Buy a piece of jewelry to symbolize the self you want to be. This does not have to be an expensive item, but it should be something that you like well enough to wear every day. Next, find a small paper or cloth bag. Now, close your eyes and hold the piece of jewelry in your hands. Caress it with your fingers. Memorize its every nook and cranny. Put it to your lips and kiss it. Say:

> **My child; my self; my lost and forgotten**
> **I conceive you now, this night**
> **Grow and thrive with life anew**
> **'Til the time for birth is right**

Carefully place your piece of jewelry into the small cloth or paper bag, and put it under your pillow. This will serve as the "womb."

### Days Two through Six

Each day, gather something to "feed" the baby. These items should be something that bring enjoyment or have personal meaning to you. Some ideas might include a small stone or crystal, a snippet of lace, soft fabric, a ribbon, a favorite photograph, or a tiny bit of herbal potpourri tied up in lace netting. There are no rules of selection here except that the items must come from the heart and you must be willing to part with them. Place each day's feeding in the bag with the "baby" and say:

> **With every single bite you eat**
> **Gather strength and power sweet**

### Day Seven

Gather the following materials:

> The bag from under your pillow
> Incense (your choice of fragrance)
> Oil (your choice of fragrance)
> Small dish of salted water
> Purple candle anointed with oil, inscribed with "Crone"
> White candle anointed with oil, inscribed with "Twin"
>   or "Spirit Self"
> Green candle anointed with oil and inscribed with your name,
>   or "me"
> Crone cord (from the Crone Welcoming Ritual)
> White ribbon or cord the same length as the Crone cord
> 2 purple pony beads

Form a tight triangle with the candles, facing the words inward so that they touch each other. Tie the Crone cord around your waist and light the incense. Say:

> **I purify this birthing room**
> **I rid it of all gloom and doom**
> **So all that remains here ever after**
> **Is the joyous scent of love and laughter**

Light the candles and say:

> **Flames of light, flicker and merge**
> **Become one flame, one life, I urge**

**Crone, myself, and twin are one**
**As I will, so be it done**

Take the jewelry item from the bag and wrap it in the white cord.
Pass the bundle through the incense smoke and say:

**I bless you well with Air and Fire**
**Bring to me what I desire**

Sprinkle it with salt-water and say:

**You I bless with Water and Earth**
**Be filled with magical value and worth**

Then hold it in your hands and close your fingers around it. Offer
it skyward and say:

**We give you birth, the Crone and I**
**We give you air to breathe**
**The fires of passion we ignite**
**Now from the womb, take leave**
**We give you water sweet to drink**
**We give you room to grow**
**We give you earth, dig deep your roots**
**Into the ground below**
**Stir now from your resting place**
**My Spirit Self, so dear**
**Rub your eyes, shake off the sleep**
**Emerge now without fear**
**Find safety in our loving arms**
**And be just who you are**
**Grow, be strong, start life anew**
**By Earth, Moon, sun, and star**
**Merge with me just as the Crone**
**Make me full and whole**
**Take your place within my life**
**And live within my soul**

Thread a pony bead on each end of the Spirit cord (white cord). Tie a knot below each one to secure it. Remove the Crone cord from your waist. Place both cords on the altar along with the jewelry, womb and feedings. Let the candles burn down completely.

## Day Eight

Gather the following materials and take them to your altar:

> Incense and oil (your choice of fragrance)
> Small dish of salted water
> 1 teaspoon each of powdered sage, rosemary, and clove
> White candle anointed with oil
> Green cord or ribbon, same length as the Crone and Spirit cords
> Tiny lock of your hair
> Sheet of newspaper

Light the incense and say:

> **Incense smoke, protect this place**
> **Fill it with your hazy grace**
> **Seal this room of total birth**
> **In love and laughter, joy and mirth**

Spread the sheet of newspaper out on the altar, and place the herbs within reach. Sprinkle the herbs over the newspaper one at a time, beginning with the sage.

As you sprinkle the sage, say:

> **For the Crone, I add this sage**
> **It brings to light the gifts of age**

Sprinkle the rosemary on top of the sage, saying:

> **For the Spirit, I add rosemary**
> **It awakens the woman I'm meant to be**

Add the clove, saying:

> **This clove is added now for me**
> **I'm the spice that blends our harmony**

Mix the herbs well with your fingers, then roll the candle in the mixture until it's well coated. Light the candle and say:

> **As this flame burns ever higher**
> **I am reborn within the fire**
> **Crone, myself, and Spirit, one**
> **The final birthing has begun**

Fold the green cord in half to find the center, then tie a lock of your hair in that spot. Pass the cord through the incense smoke, saying:

> **I am reborn of Air and Fire**
> **I am now what I desire**

Sprinkle it with the salt water, saying:

> **I am reborn of Earth and Sea**
> **I am what I was born to be**

Then gather the Crone, Spirit, and Self (green) cords together, and secure them with a knot about three inches from one end. Braid the three together while chanting:

> **Cords of beauty, cords of strength**
> **Cords of my own body length**
> **Weave us well and weave us fast**
> **Weave us into one at last**
> **I am reborn as I should be**
> **Strong and wise, complete and free**

Continue to braid to the last three inches of the cords, then knot them together securely.

Tie the cord around your waist and say:

> **I wear the cords of my rebirth**
> **As a symbol of my power and worth**
> **I release my past; it's over and done**
> **My new life has just begun**

Take the womb and feedings outside and bury them on your property. If this is not possible, bury them in a potted plant in your house. As you bury the bag, say:

> **I return this excess to the Earth**
> **I give it back in love and mirth**
> **I give you back this part of me**
> **To help you thrive, Earth; blessed be**

Wear the piece of jewelry as a symbol of your rebirth. The Rebirth cord will be used in every ritual from this point on, so put it in a safe place. Then, for each ritual, tie it around your waist before you begin, and store it again when you finish.

# Spiritual House Cleaning

Now that we've been reborn, it's time to go to work. We have to develop an environment conducive to nurturing, growth, and well-being. We have to create a situation in which the Spirit Self feels comfortable enough to communicate and interact with you and the Crone again.

Creating such an environment isn't difficult. All we have to do is get back to the spiritual basics, using their power to fertilize our lives and bring us into balance. Once in balance, we can complete the personal cycle, reach full potential, and become totally fulfilled as women.

## Balancing Personality and Character Traits

Solid spiritual construction starts with who we really are. This has nothing to do with outward appearance. What we look like only identifies us as separate beings. It's our personality and character traits that set us apart as true individuals. We each think and react differently to certain situations. What may cause one person to laugh might make another one cry. An incident that forces one person to action might cause another to flee. That's because our personalities and character traits are, to a large degree, based on how we feel about things and how we respond emotionally to any given set of circumstances.

The way we handle our feelings has a lot to do with our experiences during childhood: a time when our spirituality was still unblemished and active. The Analyst really shines here, because She knows those experiences so intimately. She's played with them, dissected them, and used them to Her best advantage. And while we weren't looking, She shaped them into self-destructing time bombs, causing dysfunctionalism in our lives and stifling our emergence as total women.

For example, the Analyst delights in turning a childhood lesson about sharing into a struggle with extreme jealousy. She revels in using one bad experience with someone of another culture to breed uncontrollable racist thoughts and ideas. She loves to point out that we're working too hard at something we'll probably never accomplish, and is ecstatic when we don't strive to reach our full potential. After all, it's easy for Her to run over lazy folks who lack initiative and the courage of their convictions.

Because of the Analyst's developmental power over us, we all have a unique blend of personality flaws, character imbalances, and particular traits that we're not necessarily proud of. We know that certain emotional responses are not socially acceptable, so we go through life suppressing our true feelings. Handling life in this fashion is a little like trying to cover the smell of a wet dog with a hefty dose of perfume. It just doesn't work. But it is within our grasp to change our negative feelings into something positive, life-enhancing, and personally empowering.

## ❖ Using the Elements as Ammunition: A Monthly Exercise

One of the best ways disarm the Analyst and repair our emotional damage is to come into balance with the Elements. Though we don't often think about it, our emotions constantly feed upon their positive and negative poles. The goal is to keep our emotions in healthy balance, for when our emotional systems absorb too much of one Element or not enough of another, things go awry. We become psychologically out of sorts as the Element imbalance causes us to lean toward negative feelings and unsavory character traits. Each Element impacts the traits that it corresponds to, as follows:

| | |
|---|---|
| **Air** | Traits involving inspiration, thought, and communication |
| **Fire** | Traits involving productivity, activity, enthusiasm, and attitude |
| **Water** | Traits involving emotions and emotional responsiveness |
| **Earth** | Traits involving dedication, practicality, trust, and capacity for nurturing |

The first step toward achieving harmony with the Elements is to recognize and list your positive and negative aspects. Be brutally honest with yourself, and don't be ashamed to write something down. Here's an example:

| Positive | Negative |
|----------|----------|
| Enthusiastic | Stubborn |
| Practical | Lazy |
| Loving | Jealous |
| Creative | Moody |
| Generous | Retaliatory |
| Honest | Irritable |
| Patient | Analytical |

After your lists are complete, take a few moments to contemplate the Elements. Ask yourself the following questions: What properties distinguish one Element from another? How do the positive and negative aspects of each Element affect your personality? Which of your character traits specifically relate to Air? Fire? Water? Earth?

With these questions in mind, make a general list for each Element, writing down all the characteristics you can think of under its related Element. This time, don't limit yourself to characteristics that you feel are definitive of your own personality. You may want to use the definitions of the Elements provided on page 24 to complete this task. If you like, start with the charts provided below and simply add to them as more attributes come to mind.

|  | Positive | Negative |
|---|----------|----------|
| **Air** | Kindness, optimism, cheerfulness, joy, diligence, adroitness | Lack of stamina, contempt, dishonesty, gossiping, fickleness, slyness |
| **Fire** | Activity, enthusiasm, eagerness, resolution, courage, productivity | Destruction, jealousy, irritability, passion, intemperance, anger |

**Water**   Devotion, modesty,                Indifference, apathy,
            compassion, calmness,              shyness, laziness,
            forgiveness, tenderness            depression, moodiness

**Earth**   Endurance, respectability,         Unreliability, dullness
            seriousness, punctuality,          cynicism, tardiness,
            confidence, responsibility         unscrupulousness,
                                               laziness

When no more traits come to mind, go back to your positive and negative character traits lists and note the related Element beside each character trait as shown below. Total each Element's appearance to determine your personal imbalance.

| Positive | Negative |
|---|---|
| Enthusiastic (Fire) | Stubborn (Earth) |
| Practical (Earth) | Lazy (Earth) |
| Loving (Water) | Jealous (Fire) |
| Creative (Air) | Moody (Water) |
| Generous (Earth) | Retaliatory (Fire) |
| Honest (Earth) | Irritable (Fire) |
| Patient (Earth) | Analytical (Air) |

Calculation of the above example shows us that Earth far outweighs the rest of the Elements, and that Water and Air in particular have very little prominence. Element totals in this example equal six Earth, four Fire, two Water, and two Air.

Bringing the Elements into balance is important for several reasons. For one, a harmonious Element blend aids in healing old emotional wounds while repairing the damage done by the Analyst. It also helps us to locate our personal strengths and weaknesses. In finding our strengths, we can utilize them better in our magic. Knowing our weaknesses is of benefit, too. Once we know where they lie, we can more easily correct them or guard against them.

Achieving Elemental balance isn't as difficult as it may seem. If your character trait list is unbalanced, then the simple act of adding certain Element-related activities to your life can quickly bring you back into sync. You should only focus on the Elements that are weakest in your personal aspects chart. Trying to combat the Elements that overpower your personality tends to make them even stronger. The idea here is not to attempt to change your personal nature but to balance the flow of the four Elements within you, all the while stealing the Analyst's power. Practical activity examples follow:

**Air**  To correct a weakness in this area, scent your house or your clothes, write letters, or meditate. Other activities might include a visit to the art museum, a friendly game of cards, or dancing to your favorite music. Do something just for fun.

**Fire**  To remedy a lack of this Element, bake sweets, warm yourself by a crackling fire, or take a brisk walk in the sunshine. Take the initiative to finish a long forgotten project or to start one you've never gotten around to.

**Water**  Activities for strengthening Water traits within yourself might include walking in the rain, taking a bubblebath, swimming, or wading through a creek. Go outside and toast the Full Moon with a glass of water, give someone a hug or, if something's been bothering you for a while, have a good, long cry.

**Earth**  To remedy a lack of this Element, work in the garden, dig a new flower bed, re-pot your houseplants or clean your house. Play with pets, start a new exercise program, hug a tree, or walk barefoot through the grass. You'll be grounded before you know it.

Do the chosen strengthening exercises for a month, and then make a new list of personal character traits without looking at the first. Compare the two when you are finished. The new list will most definitely reflect qualities that didn't appear on the last one. These additional qualities will put you more in balance. Don't be surprised in the least if you begin to feel differently about certain situations, or if you suddenly feel compelled to make radical changes in your lifestyle. All it means is that the Analyst is losing ground. And when that happens, you know that the real you, the total woman, is on the road to victory.

## Vacuuming Away Emotional Dust Bunnies

Life is full of little annoyances. Many of them seem trivial, such as a toothpaste tube squeezed from the middle instead of the bottom, a cap left off the shampoo, or a pair of shoes thrown on the living room floor. Still, they bother us. This isn't to say that we should respond to them by throwing a wall-eyed fit. To do so might cause us to appear self-centered, unbalanced, and maybe even fit for the loony bin. Instead, we spend a good portion of our time righting the things that make us crazy. What we don't realize is that our temporary fixes are just that: temporary. They don't really solve a thing. Our aggravation just builds up until we're hopping, seething mad, with an attitude the size of the Grand Canyon. Decidedly, this is emotionally unhealthy. That's not the worst of it, though. Left to fester, this negative energy can actually clog the communication flow between our spiritual and physical realms, and undo all the hard work we've put toward creating a positive environment.

The most effective way to safeguard against this is to keep a daily journal. Don't worry if you don't have anything profound to say. This isn't that kind of journal. Nothing you write in it will impact society, change humankind, or make the collective world a better place to live. In fact, unless you leave it lying around, it will probably never be seen by another pair of human eyes.

Journal writing is one of the best things you can do for yourself. It provides a place where you can air your dirty laundry, bitch at the world, and even scream at the Ancients if you take a notion. It sucks up negative thought patterns and ideas quicker than you can say "Goddess," and totally clears the channels of communication between the spiritual and physical realms. It removes everything except positive energy, and leaves you with a fresh perspective, a good attitude, and the power to realize your dreams. What could be better?

## The Daily Journal: Getting Started

The hardest part of keeping the daily journal is getting started. The reasons for putting it off are varied and numerous. Some people insist that they have no problems, gripes, or bitches. Others simply think that they have nothing to say. The most common reason of all, though, is that there just isn't enough time to keep a journal. Hogwash! No one's life is perfect, we all have something to say, and no matter how busy our life is, each of us makes time for the things that we think are important.

The time you spend writing in your journal is the most important time you'll spend every day. Why? Because it's one of the most powerful, life-changing tools available. As you write, synchronicity comes into play. Small problems seem to evaporate into thin air. The tougher ones somehow manage to solve themselves. Without a bunch of obstacles in the way, life becomes new, fresh, and exciting. It's like having a blank canvas to decorate with a brand new reality— any reality you like!

All you need to get started is determination, a pen and some paper, or your computer. Begin writing as soon after you wake up as possible. The brain is still a bit hazy then, and you're less likely to cover up any negative feelings. There aren't any rules. Write whatever you want. If you don't know what to write, write that until you think of something else. The idea is to keep writing whatever happens to pop into your mind, as quickly as you can get it down. Do this without stopping for at least two pages. Once you get the hang of it, you'll be surprised at how easily the words flow.

Still not sure about how this works? Maybe it will help to take a look at one of my early journal entries:

> *I don't know what to write. How could I? I have writer's block. This is ridiculous. I'm sick of things that waste my time. I need to go the store today. Wonder if I have any eggs? Is the milk gone? The dog is whining to go out. Should I take her? I think I'll wait. I shouldn't be interrupted right now. This is supposed to be important. They say it'll change my life. I still think it's pretty silly . . .*

There's nothing profound or earth-shattering here. In fact, it closely resembles psycho-babble. But that doesn't matter. What *does* matter is that this exercise clears out the superfluous junk meandering through your brain, allowing you to focus on what's important. Your life. Its potential. And, of course, your dreams. There's nothing more important than that.

## Meditation: The Cosmic Conference Call

The art of meditation has been around for centuries, but it enjoyed a grand resurgence during the peace movement of the 1960s. Since that time, it's become an important part of many spiritual paths. The reason for its popularity has to do with the versatility of the art.

Meditation can be used for personal relaxation, for connecting and transferring energies, and to channel messages from the spirit world. It's a great grounding tool for people with scattered and sporadic energies, and works wonders for others who need to summon self-confidence and courage. Its most common use, though, has to do with gaining focus, insight, and solutions to difficult problems.

Meditation is important during menopause because it allows you to communicate with all three phases of yourself at once: personal Crone, Spirit Self, and Crone twin. It works a little like a cosmic conference call. You can ask questions, get answers, and gain insight. You can make decisions based on the input of all three parties. Best of all, you can make sure that everyone is happy, and that no one is feeling ignored or left out.

Daily meditation ensures a smooth transition into the Crone's world. Don't worry about working it into your busy schedule. Fifteen minutes before bedtime is all you need. Don't worry about the privacy issue. Meditation doesn't require a lot of room and doesn't create a spectacle. If privacy is a problem, you can always meditate in the bathtub. When it comes to meditation, the "when" and "where" is not important. The only thing that matters is that you do it.

If you've never meditated before, a set of quick-start instructions is outlined below for your convenience. Give them a whirl—get started today. It's the best guarantee you can have toward great spiritual communication and a happy beginning in your new life.

## ❖ How to Meditate

1. Sit in a comfortable position. This doesn't mean you have to sit cross-legged on the floor. "Comfortable" is whatever feels good to you. This might mean sitting in a recliner, on the bed, or even at the kitchen table.

2. Close your eyes and relax.

3. Silently repeat the word "I" over and over to yourself. Pay close attention to the sound of the word and to the sound of your breath as you inhale and exhale.

4. Don't get upset if other thoughts enter your mind or get in the
   way. Just dismiss them and turn your focus back to the word "I"
   and the natural flow of your breathing.

You may not hear from the Crone or the Spirit Self the first few times
you meditate. This is common. Just learn the routine and let it
become a natural part of you. Once you do, they'll surface. And once
they surface, you may never get a word in edgewise again!

# Chapter 2

# If I'd Known Then What I Know Now

No matter how distraught I was about the Crone phase at the onset, I did look forward to one of its benefits: reaching the age that brought wisdom. I'd spent years wanting it, waiting for it and, at last, I was going to have it. I daydreamed about helping people turn their lives around with just one sage word or two. Just thinking about it made me smile.

"Wipe that silly grin off your face. It makes you look like a dullard!" She-Who-Nags, true to form, had dropped by to give me Her daily dose of aggravation.

"And a good morning to You, too, dear Crone!" I kept the smile on my face, just for fun.

"Real wisdom has nothing to do with age. It's living, doing, and remembering."

"What?!"

"Look back on your life. Reflect for a while. You'll see."

She-Who-Nags was right. It occurred to me that people had been asking my advice for as long as I could remember. While I certainly didn't have all the answers, I hadn't done badly. I was blessed with a level head, could look at things objectively, and had the ability to criticize constructively. I also knew when something was out of my league. What I'd been dreaming about for so many years had come to pass while I wasn't looking. Wisdom, or at least the initial stages of it, was already mine.

The point is, real wisdom has nothing to do with how old we are. It's a matter of how much we've lived, what we've experienced, and how we've dealt with the consequences. Sure, we make mistakes along the way. But that's how we learn. Folks who don't make mistakes aren't really living. They're only watching their lives go by. Real life is a trial and error process, and we spend most of it figuring out what works and what doesn't.

Regret has no place in wisdom gathering. It's a waste of time to ponder things that are impossible to change. Real wisdom comes from remembering previous consequences, avoiding risky situations, and refusing to repeat past mistakes. It comes from being able to look at the big picture (the cosmic plan), and to then work out our problems to the benefit of everyone concerned. But most of all, it comes from listening and acting according to your inner voice: the voice of your personal Crone.

## Wisdom Gathering, Crone-Style

One of the best things I ever did for myself was decide to listen to She-Who-Nags. Her wise-cracking, smart-alecky ways aside, She saved me tons of time and energy in the wisdom-gathering department.

When I asked Her how to obtain total wisdom, She provided me with a wonderful plan. It outlined the aspects of myself that I needed to embrace and develop, including creation, growth, universal acknowledgment, personal identity, balance, perspective, healing, release, and unconditional love. For each aspect, She-Who-Nags gave me an appropriate meditation, affirmation, and an exercise with which to work. Before long, I was firmly footed on the right path and happily collecting pearls of wisdom every step of the way.

# ❖ Wisdom Gathering Exercises

She-Who-Nags' plan is outlined below for your convenience. There's no right or wrong way to work through this process, but I find it easier to record myself reading the meditation so I have a tape to guide my journey. After the meditation, I follow with the affirmation, and then go on to the practical exercise. If you have trouble pouring energy into the exercise, try working only with the meditation and affirmation for a few days. Then try the exercise again.

## 1. Creation

Most of us think the creation process belongs only to the young. It's just not so. Birth and creation are very important parts of wisdom gathering. They come in the form of rediscovery, and that's what menopause is really all about. It's a birthing process—a rite of passage—and the baby in question is you.

If we don't realize this from the beginning, it's easy to become confused and upset. Suddenly we feel differently about things. Views that we've held for years may now get tossed aside and exchanged for ideas that are alien to our previous way of thinking. Our priorities may change, too, and what used to be important might now seem trivial. We become brand new women with fresh ideas, different goals, and far-reaching dreams. There's no need to be alarmed. It's just the process of creation at work.

This form of creation is much different from any we've ever experienced. It causes us to look at each day with new wonder and hope. It makes us aware of fresh opportunities and unlimited possibilities. And in that heightened awareness, we acquire the courage to move forward, to make changes, and to reach out and grab what we most desire. The Crone gives us the incentive to change our personal reality and exchange it for something better. She allows us to create the reality we see in our dreams.

## Meditation

It is dawn and the Sun is just starting to break through the nighttime black with a blaze of color. With bare feet, I walk across a meadow dotted with the green verdancy of new sprouts. I smell the richness of damp black soil all around me and feel its soft warmth cushioning my every step. Singing birds flit here and there, carrying bits of straw and moss for nest-building. The air is filled with the sounds of Nature. Crickets chirp. Horses neigh. Squirrels chatter with joy as they shinny up and down the trees and frolic with each other.

As the sky fills with light, I see a figure up ahead. It's a middle-aged woman. She walks alone and, as she walks, she studies the wild flower in her hand. Finally, she pauses, lifts the flower to her nose, and inhales deeply. At that moment, a great transformation occurs. The years that aged her fall away quickly, one after another, until she reaches pre-pubescent girlhood once more.

Sunlight shines on her face, enhancing its radiant beauty. Her eyes filled with wonder, she looks at her surroundings as if she's seeing them for the very first time. She tosses the flower on the morning breeze. As it floats to the ground, the entire meadow bursts into vibrant blossom. She turns to face me, a look of knowing and experience in her eyes.

## Affirmation

**I am fresh and new—I am wild and free
I can be anything I want to be,
because I know what the young do not
I have the experience to create my plot**

## Exercise

Think of two small changes and one large one that you'd like to make in your life this week. Write each one on a small piece of paper and tape them to something you'll see every day. The bathroom mirror or refrigerator are usually good spots. Think creatively and take active steps to make the changes. Burn the appropriate papers as the goals manifest in reality.

Repeat this exercise until your personal reality is exactly the way that you have envisioned.

# 2. Growth

Growth is a difficult aspect to accept because it involves change. It upsets the plans we've laid out for ourselves. It messes with all that is stable, focused, and dependable in our lives. In short, it turns our control over to some unseen force. And, for most of us, losing that control is one of the scariest things we can imagine. Still, as bad as personal growth seems at the onset, its rewards will always outweigh its aggravations.

Such is the way with menopause, which is the most important growth process that we, as women, experience. Yes, our bodies change, but it's more than that. Much more. It marks the time in our lives when we really come into our own. It allows us to change our course, become who we are, and embark upon an adventure of total fulfillment. All we have to do is cooperate.

All personal growth takes cooperation. To get the most from it, we have to face our fears and go forward. So what if we make a mistake or two along the way? Our errors aren't nearly as significant as we think; nothing's so bad it can't be rectified later. So what if we aren't sure which path to take? No problem. Explore them all. Embrace the adventure and enjoy the fun along the way. There's plenty to be had.

Because nothing grows without fertilizer, we also need to learn to nurture ourselves just as much as we nurture those around us. This means forgiving our personal shortcomings, resting when we're tired, and allowing ourselves to just be. Once we learn to be as generous with ourselves as we are with others, our limits fall by the wayside and we bud and blossom into the women we were meant to be.

## Meditation

The stirrings of summer's warmth are in the air, and the midday sun shines brightly on my back as I meander through the park. I marvel at the lush green of the trees and grass, and the flowering abundance that spills forth from every nook and cranny. I stop at the pond to feed the resident ducks and geese. They gobble happily at the sandwich bits offered from my picnic basket. Then I travel on, looking for the perfect spot to eat lunch.

As I walk, I spot a small grove of oak trees. I hurry in that direction, for the trees seem to be calling to me, inviting me to leave the path and share the coolness of their shade. I reach the grove, spread a blanket, and prepare to eat. Then I hear it. The wail of a small child.

I look up to see a little girl wandering about. She's lost and confused. The sting of a bee has left a large red welt on her upper arm. I gather her into my arms, comfort her, and dry her tears. After the stinger is removed, I laugh and say that that her skin must be very tough to have caused that bee to lose his nose. She laughs too, feeling safe and secure at last. We share lunch. Just as I'm packing up to take her to the park station, her worried parents arrive. They hug her tightly, so happy to find her that they forget all about scolding her.

Her parents thank me, and we all leave the park much happier than we were when we entered it. I know that because of my efforts and those of her parents, the child will no longer be afraid of the changes that fall along her path.

## Affirmation

**I am growing every day in thought and word and deed**
**I welcome changes on my path; they bring me what I need**
**I no longer fear mistakes; I learn from them each day**
**They fertilize my inner core as I grow on my way**

## Exercise

Try something new today—anything you want. Taste a new food. Sample a new hairstyle. Wear something completely out of character. Do something fun that you've never had the gumption to try. Don't worry that your choice might be a mistake. If it is, you can always fix it tomorrow. Have fun for today. Enjoy your new experience.

# 3. Universal Acknowledgment

This aspect of wisdom gathering isn't nearly as difficult to embrace as some others on the list. Why? Because most of us believe in a higher power. The universe is relative to that power and just as sacred. It encompasses all that is space, from countless galaxies to the narrow area that connects us to a deity. It's a spiritual collective that watches as we walk our paths, sees us as we strive to reach our goals, and tosses out treats and aggravations along the way. It is the starting point from which we all begin and the place where we all connect to one another as siblings. It's the all-seeing, all-knowing place where energies join, move, and transform. It is the place where real magic is born.

The universe is like a large spider web and we each have a personal strand in its structure. To a large degree, our placement in the universal web determines the personal life lessons we must learn to evolve spiritually. It connects us to those who can help us reach our goals. It connects us to those who can ease our life lessons. It defines our personal roles within the universal plan, provides us with a support system, and gives us an incentive to move forward. In short, it defines individual existence on this plane and gives our lives purpose.

Universal acknowledgment sets us apart from others because it causes us to look beyond ourselves. It forces us to look toward the future rather than at the present, to evaluate the big picture instead of only considering our tiny personal portions. And, as we embrace it, we suddenly discover that everything we do and every action we take affects the existence of everyone else in the web. We realize that one person not only *can* make a difference, but *does* make a difference.

## Meditation

It is dawn and the world is just awakening to the new day. Birds sing. Squirrels chatter. The cat down the street stretches and yawns. I wake up, too, and slowly begin to stir along my path. I sense something different in the air. Something new and exciting. Then I look down. The difference is in my path. It is changing . . . not in direction, but in form. The damp earth beneath my feet transforms itself into a glistening silver strand. The morning Sun shines upon the crystal gardens that line its sides and casts random rainbows of color here and there. It's a beautiful sight, and I hurry along to see what's ahead of me.

Suddenly, I'm transported out of my body and lifted high above my path. I look down and watch myself scurry along, doing what I need to do, tending to the things I must. Then I see the total picture. It's a giant web that covers the Earth, each path connecting to the next, each connection completing the whole. I notice the people on the paths connected directly to mine. I know them. They're my friends. My acquaintances. My loved ones.

I watch as they move toward their goals, and see how my actions affect their every step. I realize that nothing in this life happens by chance, and that everyone I meet along my way is introduced to me for a reason. I understand that my personal strand in the web plays an integral role in the lives of those around me, and exists to complete the universal plan. I see that the plan depends on me and the choices I make. I am important. I make a difference. By my very existence, I make the world a better place to live.

## Affirmation

**I respond well to the universe and to its plan for me**
**I see the bigger picture and how it sets us free**
**I accept my strand within its web,**
**its gifts, its joys and sorrows**
**I embrace its wisdom now to secure**
**a better world tomorrow**

## Exercise

Make a trip to the nearest pond. If that's not an option, fill your bathtub half full of water. Toss in a pebble and see what happens. Watch as the force of the pebble causes rings of ripples. They begin in the center and work outward. This is how your actions affect others in the universal web. Know that everything you do affects someone else, and that everything you do makes a difference.

## 4. Personal Identity

Though it may seem similar, this aspect has little to do with the strand we hold in the universal web. Identity is who we are, not what we do. It's a complex combination of the experiences, ideas, and feelings we've gathered from this life and from those we've lived before.

This personal combination is what forms us as individual people and makes us unlike anyone else on the planet. Because it's human nature to conform to the expectations of others, some of us spend a lot of time trying to "fit in." We struggle toward whatever is currently fashionable, popular, and politically correct. We desperately try to emulate those we admire and respect. But at the end, all our efforts are for naught. We just wind up miserable and more confused than ever.

Personal identity is like a kaleidoscope: multi-faceted and ever-changing. Each day of our lives fills us with new experiences and emotions. No one is the same person tomorrow as they are today, and that's okay. It just means that we cannot be forced into a mold of someone else's choosing, nor should we try.

We must learn to accept whomever we are on any given day, and to embrace ourselves with the love and understanding that we deserve. In doing so, we allow ourselves the freedom of growth and transformation. We allow ourselves to become the best persons we can possibly be.

## Meditation

It is a crisp, cool autumn day and the wind stirs briskly all around me. It licks at my nose, blows through my hair, and twirls through the leaves that fall to the ground. I stop and listen for a moment. I hear its message. It speaks of change, individuality, movement, and transformation. I smile in understanding and move forward, excited to explore the tiny village ahead.

I stop along the cobblestone road and wander through the shops that strike my fancy. Suddenly, I spot a store set apart from the others. Even though the building is rather plain and there's no sign outside, I know it's a special place. I walk through the door and enter a room filled with magical hats.

Each hat is labeled with its properties, its physical attributes, and its mental attitudes. As I try them on, I change into the people they represent. Mother. Lover. Teacher. Artist. Politician. Religious figure. But even in my changing, I still see a part of myself—a part that is different from my friends—a part that is who I always will be.

As I leave, the wind twirls about me, whispering its message. I realize that we all play many different roles in this life, and it is my unique combination of roles that makes me who I am. I understand that the roles I play are ever-growing and ever-changing, and that I cannot be tomorrow the person that I am today. I know that I am precisely who I should be at every moment in my life.

## Affirmation

**I am free to be just who I am at any point in time**
**I live the aspects of myself within the cosmic rhyme**
**Teacher, mother, lover, friend; all these belong to me**
**It matters not what you expect; I am who I should be**

## Exercise

Gather together photographs of yourself at different stages in your life. Begin with some of you as a baby, and continue gathering until you find a recent one. Look back on your life. Then make a list of all the roles you've claimed since birth. Study the photos carefully, paying close attention to the eyes. See the wisdom of experience in them— the wisdom gathered from your special combination of roles. Know that this is what makes you uniquely different from everyone else. This is what makes you special.

## 5. Balance

All of us learned about opposites in school. Right and wrong. Good and bad. Man and woman. Dark and light. We really didn't give it much thought back then. All we knew was that each attracted its contrasting force as readily as a magnet drew up metal. There was no further explanation necessary. We were children and that was enough.

As we grow older, though, we realize there's more to the balancing act than the attraction of opposites. We discover that our lives are governed by the laws of checks and balances. For every debit, there must be sufficient credit. For every reward, a sacrifice. For every tear, the warmth of a smile. Once we understand that balance is the key to life, our lives become easier. Problems don't seem as insurmountable because we know there's a solution hiding nearby. We view obstacles and challenges more readily as chances and opportunities. Accepting life's little aggravations rather than dwelling on them definitely makes us happier, more productive people. But that's not all. It brings synchronicity into play and introduces us to spiritual balance: that gentle harmony we've been striving for all along.

## Meditation

I feel the chill of autumn's breeze as I stand in the market place. Merchant canopies line the streets and the town buzzes with activity. I have not come to sell my wares. I have come to purchase apples, for they are the fruit of balanced wisdom. I search each fruit stall carefully, but there are no apples to be found. Not to be discouraged, I move on. I stop and inquire at every booth. The response is always negative. When I reach the last canopy, though, my efforts are rewarded. The merchant proudly displays the object of my search. He smiles as he holds up two baskets of apples. They are the only two baskets to be had in the entire market, and they don't look very good. Some are bruised. Some are wormy. Even worse, the price is high. I start to leave but, remembering my mission, I reconsider. I pay the man and head for home.

After sorting the fruit, I discover that only half the apples are edible. I eat one apple and can the rest. Then I bury the spoiled ones in the back yard. Thunder rumbles overhead. The skies open up and sheets of rain pour forth. I rush inside, dry myself by the fire, and go to bed.

The next morning, I look outside. Much to my surprise, there are changes in the pile of rotten fruit and dirt. Even in their waste, they have sprouted green with new life and fresh possibility.

## Affirmation

**I understand that obstacles are chances in disguise,
and that life is full of opposites like sun and moonlit skies
I jump the hurdles in my life, I laugh, and I feel pain
I walk the road of balanced life; it brings me spiritual gain**

## Exercise

Write down three unpleasant events that altered your life. Think about them one at a time and remember them in detail. Write them out on paper if you like. Now look objectively at the long-range changes they caused, and the opportunities that came your way because of them. Do the positive changes balance with the negative ones? Don't be surprised if they actually outweigh any unpleasantness you felt at the onset.

## 6. Perspective

Perspective is the way we look at life and view how its events relate to us. It can often be a difficult aspect to develop properly. Why? Because we tend to hang on to the same old ideas and thoughts on every subject imaginable. It's not that we're blind to the things going on around us. It's not that we don't realize it's time to listen, learn, and change our views. It's just that our old ideas are familiar, comfortable and, like an old pair of jeans, easy to wear.

Our world is in a constant state of flux, and we need to learn to change with it. This doesn't mean that we should give up our personal codes of ethics, our belief systems, or our deepest, truest feelings. It does mean that we should examine why we feel and think the way we do and strive to rid ourselves of the negativity that clutters our minds. Once that negative energy is gone, the need to ask "why" lessens, and we give our minds the ability to check into life's "why not's." Only then can we open ourselves to fresh ideas, new possibilities, and the opportunities they present.

## Meditation

I live in the heart of the forest beside a rippling stream. I am strong, lithe, and beautiful, and spend my time dancing with the wind. My best friends are the forest animals and I am in perfect harmony with Nature. I am part of it. I am a willow tree.

Even though I am happy in the forest, I long to be like my neighbor. She is stronger than I. Taller than I. She is a striking figure: serene and intimidating all at once. While I frivolously dance in the wind, she stands perfectly still. Ever-watching. Ever-knowing. Ever-peaceful. She is the oak. And to be like her, I must learn to be still.

One day, though, the winds begin to blow and the urge to dance overtakes my vow to be still. The harder they blow, the faster I dance. They blow faster, wilder, and freer then I ever imagined. I keep their rhythm, and continue to move until I become the winds and they become me.

Then, through the dance, I hear a ripping, cracking sound. Afterward, a loud thud. I look up to see the oak, who, in her still and peaceful inflexibility, has fallen to the ground.

## Affirmation

> **I change my vision to reflect that which ought to be**
> **I have no limits—I give myself to new possibilities**
> **I embrace each fresh idea that runs across my mind**
> **I'm flexible; I accept change—my life begins to shine**

## Exercise

Without reading the articles, scan the headlines from any popular tabloid magazine. Mark any that evoke strong, personal feelings, then pick one. Focusing only on the headline, ask yourself these questions: What does the headline mean to you? What story would you expect to follow the heading? What exactly in that phrase makes an impact on you?

When you're finished, read the article. Did the headline capture the true contents of the article? After reading the article, do you feel the same way you did when you first saw the headline? Don't be surprised if the answers to both questions are "no." It's just a change of perspective at work.

Now, find a lengthy headline from the same magazine. Mix up the words and see how many other headlines you can make from it. Notice how many different meanings you can communicate with the same set of words, and how quickly your perspective changes with an alteration in word placement.

## 7. Healing

Most of us associate the powers of healing with doctors, dentists, and psychologists. It's mostly because of our upbringing. We grow up thinking that the doctor can fix whatever ails us. We grow up thinking that "doctor" is synonymous with "God" or "Goddess." Even worse, we grow up thinking that personal health is the one area of life over which we have no control.

Surprisingly enough, we probably have more control over our health than any other area in our lives. It all has to do with free will and personal choices. We can choose to eat right, exercise, and get plenty of rest. We can choose to control our emotions instead of letting them run away with us. We can choose to have safe sex and live drug-free lives. In doing so, we bolster the immune system and reinforce a positive outlook on life. It's the first step toward keeping disease at bay.

Disease only creeps in when we let our guard down. When that happens, the doctor can be of use; after all, doctors have medical training that we don't. But even an army of doctors can't heal us all by themselves. They need our help, because maintaining good health is a joint effort. Without our cooperation, all the medicine in the world won't fix what ails us.

So, how do we cooperate? We brandish the most valuable weapon we have, a positive attitude, and use it to strike back. Stress, depression, and despair are the culprits that open the door for disease. While it's hard to completely remove them from our lives, it's easy to not invite them in. All we have to do is choose to be in a good mood rather than a bad one, learn from our mistakes instead of repeating them, and insist on being happy instead of sad. Above all, learn to smile. A smile goes a long way toward cementing a positive attitude. Besides, it's more contagious than any disease!

## Meditation

I travel through my body, mind, and spirit in search of intruding disease. I know it's there. I feel it. I smell it. I hear its destructive force hard at work. I travel through hills and valleys, oceans and plains. I search out every nook and cranny of my being. At long last, I see the intruder. It's come in the form of a brilliant red ooze. I watch as its poison spreads and slowly invades my system.

I reach into my bag of weapons and retrieve a can of magical spray. I pull off the cap, take aim, and give it a shot. The soft, green color of health begins to replace the red offender. It's only a mist at first. After a while, though, the green becomes rich, even, and stronger than the red. The disease runs this way and that, trying to escape. Finally, it has no choice but to leave my being. As the disease evaporates, its malignant energy is transformed into something positive, healthy, and beneficial. It joins with the green of health to form a protective bandage and guard against further intrusion.

**Affirmation**

I have the power to heal myself:
my body, mind, and spirit
It grows strong within my deepest core;
All negative entities fear it
It eliminates trouble and confusion,
germs, stress, and disease
Whenever I have the need to heal,
I call it forth with ease

**Exercise**

There's a good reason for the old adage, "An apple a day keeps the doctor away." Apples are magical. When sliced crosswise, a pentagram appears at the center. They also contain a positive charge at their core. All things considered, it's no wonder that eating an apple every day is a very healthy thing to do.

Add an apple or a glass of apple juice to your daily diet. Enchant it for good health by saying:

Magical fruit, attend to my health
Lend your positive energy's wealth
Ward off anxiety, ward off disease
As I will, so mote it be

## 8. Release

This is, perhaps, one of the most difficult lessons to deal with. We spend years trying to learn to let go of stressful situations, unhealthy relationships, and lots of other things we can't fix. Somehow, we manage to justify their release in our minds but, when it comes right down to it, our hearts just won't allow us to give them the old heave-ho.

Why? Because letting go means losing something. A piece of us. And that makes us sad.

One of the easiest ways to let go of the nasties we accumulate is to view them as they are: yesterday's garbage. After all, they're nothing more than a byproduct of what was once useful to personal lesson-learning. They are leftovers that must be discarded and cleared away to make room for opportunity and personal growth.

Once we learn to toss these things aside, our lives become what we've always dreamed: a limitless flow of positive energy and fresh possibility.

## Meditation

It is late afternoon. The Sun begins his descent into the horizon. The colors of his daily farewell, peach and orange, violet and lavender, burst through the sky and flavor my thoughts. I reflect on my life, the roads I've traveled, the paths I've crossed, and the aftermath of my mistakes. A trash bag and broom in hand, I travel back in time. Back through yesterday's living. Back through the days before. Back through my entire life, until I reach the first day of my existence on this plane.

I turn and slowly make my way forward again. There's no need to hurry. I have plenty of time. I explore every nook and cranny, searching for problem areas, negative energy, and what must be cleared away for effective living. I toss each problem, each nuisance, and each aggravation into the bag, then carefully sweep away any related negativity. Some items I collect are bittersweet, and I stop for a moment to mourn their memories. But then I continue onward, collecting and sweeping, until finally I reach the end of today's living.

I return just as the blackness of night overtakes the sky. I knot the bag, carefully sealing away old miseries, old mistakes, and old maladies. Then, gripping the bag firmly, I hurl it into the nighttime sky. It travels upward and outward, past time and space and matter. Swallowed up by the universe, it is gone from my life forever.

As I turn my back, a breeze stirs and moves the clouds away from the Full Moon. She envelops me in light, love, and positive energy.

## Affirmation

**I cut my losses here and now, for nothing lasts forever
My heart accepts this and I know that some ties I must sever
I will grieve some for what was, and some tears may fall
But I'll come out cleansed and renewed, and stronger for it all**

## Exercise

Think of three things you need to remove from your life. These may be relationships, habits, illnesses, or any other hindrance toward a physically, mentally, and spiritually healthy life. Then get a piece of string or yarn, three feet long, and mark it into one-foot sections.

Tie one knot in the end of the string, and another just before the one foot mark. Name that section for one of the items on your list, then cut the string after the second knot, saying:

**I cut you from my life
And with you, stress and strife
Go away, you've been severed
From my life, you're gone forever**

Wad the string up in your hands and release it into a body of running water. Alternatively, bury it in the ground. Repeat the process with the other two items. Repeat this exercise whenever you have difficulties with release.

## 9. Unconditional Love

Unconditional love is not perfect love. It's not the kind of love that we find in fairy tales or in romance novels. It's not the kind of love that we share with our friends, our children, or even with our pets. In fact, it goes against the grain of everything that we've been taught love should be. Unconditional love has absolutely nothing to do with whether we like someone or approve of their attitude, let alone whether we agree with what they do. Simply put, it's a matter of allowing those around us to be who they are without personal expectation, agreement, or ramification.

Obviously, unconditional love isn't something that we're born with; it's something we have to work on and develop. The key is to learn the difference between "like" and "love."

*Like* comes from a common denominator upon which friendship is based. In a "like" relationship, each party works hard not to hurt the other. In this scenario, we will usually find ourselves in agreement with the other person's choices and, when we don't, we can easily agree to disagree.

*Love* is not the same. It means that no matter what other people do, no matter how negatively their actions affect us or how they harm or hurt us, we wish no ill to befall them. We wish them the best as they walk through life, and pray for speed along their journey. We don't worry about whether they accept responsibility for their actions. We don't worry that their actions don't meet our expectations. Instead, we open our hearts and accept them as they are. We understand that they are who they must be.

This doesn't mean, however, that we have to allow these people to constantly mess with our lives or suck up our positive energies. Sometimes the most loving thing we can do for others is to simply leave them alone. By staying away from them, we allow our offenders (and ourselves) to freely continue on a personal path, unimpaired and unencumbered.

## Meditation

It's a clear, summer morning. The sun rises quickly in the sky and, in his gentle warmth, all of Nature begins to stir. Crickets chirp happily. A whippoorwill calls sweetly to her mate, awakening me from my bed of pine needles deep in the forest. I yawn and stretch, then breathe deeply of the fresh, clean air. I rise, gather my belongings, and set off in search of nuts and berries for my morning meal.

As I reach the forest edge, I see an adjacent thicket covered with blackberry vines. The vines are heavy with fruit and beckon me onward. My mouth waters and I hurry toward them, tasting their sweetness with every step I take. Just as I reach the vines, though, I stop short. I hear a sound. A sound that strikes fear in the very core of my heart.

I look down to see a rattlesnake. Coiled to strike, she guards the vines, the object of my morning harvest. I step back. She relaxes. I step forward. She prepares to attack. The snake is old and wise. So am I. I know she is doing her job, and that she's traveling her personal path. I also understand that we can both escape injury if I retreat.

I step away from the thicket and away from the vines. I turn my back and calmly walk toward the pecan tree that grows a few feet away. As I begin to harvest the nuts, I glance over at the snake. Uncoiled and relaxed, she basks happily in the summer sun.

## Affirmation

**Expectations are not love; I shun them from my heart**
**I allow all to be who they must be to play their cosmic part**
**I freely give my love to all who wander through my path,**
**without worry of my love returned, result, or aftermath**

**Exercise**

Set aside a whole day for yourself. This means no phone calls, no shopping, no errands, etc. Get up early, pack a blanket, some snacks, and a lunch, and leave the house. Go to the beach, the woods, the mountains, or even a local park. Any easily accessible outdoor area is fine. The idea is to get away from life's normal demands and spend time by yourself.

When you reach your destination, pick a comfortable spot, spread your blanket, and just be. Watch the birds, the squirrels, the insects, or whatever wildlife is indigenous to the area. See them care for and interact with the trees, the grass, the flowers, and each other. Pay attention as the natural cycle of life unfolds before your eyes. Notice how the creatures and spirits of Nature allow each other to play their individual parts without disruption or intervention. All work together to complete the cycle, yet each is free to follow a personal path.

# Wisdom Walking

In addition to She-Who-Nags' comprehensive plan, there are other steps (so to speak) that we can take in order to achieve total wisdom. One great way, which also happens to be a healthful practice, is to bring wisdom walking into your life.

Since the beginning of time, history has portrayed its great seers and prophets on foot. No historian has ever written about them riding a camel, a horse, or, in the case of modern prophets, driving in a car. It could be argued that because most of them shunned society and its pleasures, they just couldn't afford any other sort of transportation. It's a good argument. But it just isn't so. The reason that the world's wisdom gatherers walked through life is because they were privy to something we were never taught. Wisdom can be gathered through making physical contact with the Earth. Through sitting on it. Through standing on it. But most of all, through walking on it.

As magical practitioners, we know that crystals store knowledge. We program them to help us in our magic, and count on them to "remember" their duties. From a more mundane standpoint, we also understand that these stones have a great capacity for data collection and storage. As the prime ingredient in computer chips, they hold, retrieve, process, and dispense thousands of data bytes per second. Because of their ability to store and process information, we don't have to remember so many things at once. At the touch of a finger, we can grab any bit of information we need, and we have the crystal to thank for it. Okay, but what does that have to do with the Earth, walking, and wisdom gathering?

Like the crystals we use in technology and magic, the Earth collects and dispenses data. Every time we walk, we cause an impression on the Earth. It records our personal marks and makes a copy of everything we know, everything we've learned, and everything we are. It gets better. Every time our feet touch the ground, we also become privy to other imprints. Those of every person who ever traveled over that particular piece of land. We are exposed to the personal reflections of our ancestors. We can connect with the innermost thoughts and insights of ancient cultures. In short, it gives us access to the collective wisdom of the ages. All we have to do is open our minds, reach out, and grab it. Keeping this in mind, it's easy to walk your way to answers and solutions. Here's how . . .

## ❖ Wisdom Walking Exercise

1. Go outside and ask the Earth a question. Do this silently. It keeps others from looking at you strangely.

2. Once the question is posed, just walk for twenty or thirty minutes. You don't have to walk briskly. There's no need to focus on the question. Just meander along and enjoy yourself.

3.  If answers come during the walking period, make a mental note of them. If not, don't worry. They will come within twenty-four hours of the initial query.

Walking has benefits beyond wisdom gathering, too. It's the most natural way to ground and center—and in this busy time, we can all use a quick fix to keep our energies from scattering. Even better, this type of walking can be managed during a fifteen-minute work break. When you return, you'll be much more relaxed and better able to cope with whatever the workplace doles out.

As you walk, visualize the Earth's grounding energy entering your body through the soles of your feet and traveling upward through your body to the top of your head. Then see it pushing your scattered, negative energy out through the back of your head, loosing it out on the ground and leaving it there behind you.

Don't worry about what the scattered energy might do to the Earth. It's quickly absorbed, rooted, and transformed into positive energy that can be used by humankind again and again.

Walking is also a terrific tool for uncovering past lives. How? Just as we access the Earth's collective wisdom, we can also rediscover the collective self. It doesn't matter that we may never have previously walked over the particular plot of ground we currently walk on. We do know that we have walked on some plot of ground in a previous life and that it, too, belongs to the Earth's mass. It's a simple matter of asking the Earth to locate each land mass related to the collective self, process the data, and deliver it to the conscious mind.

Past-life wisdom walking works much the same way as collective wisdom walking. Instead of formulating a complicated query, though, a simple "Who am I?" works well. Then follow steps two and three. The results will astound you.

To get the most out of wisdom walking, set some time aside for a stroll every day. You don't have to walk briskly or exert a lot of energy.

You don't have to concentrate or focus on your question or intent. You can even stop to smell the flowers, pick up a rock, or talk to the neighbor's dog.

Just put one foot in front of the other and see what happens. Not only will you gather more wisdom than you can imagine, you'll soon be well on your way to physical fitness. After all, walking strengthens the heart, tones the muscles, and eases sore joints. You might even lose an inch or two!

## Weaving Your Life through Dreams

Have you ever given much thought to why we dream? Some folks believe it's the body's way of relieving stress, of forcing us to relax, of keeping the subconscious mind involved enough to let the physical body heal. Others believe that dreams stimulate the imagination, open a channel between the mundane and the spiritual and, to a large degree, shape the people we grow to be. None of these folks are wrong. In Her infinite wisdom, though, She-Who-Nags offers another dream-related angle. She says we dream so we can change our personal reality.

Dream-weaving is a powerful magic as old as humankind, and you don't need a lot of props to guarantee effectiveness. All you need is a place to sleep, the willingness to change your life, and possibly a dream stone. Although the stone is optional, it aids the magic by providing a point of focus for the magic as well as forming a connection between you and the dream world. While the type of stone doesn't matter (it can be any stone you're drawn to), quartz crystals are a sure bet for dream work. They retain information, are easy to program, and can help you to remember your dreams.

## Cleansing and Programming the Dream Stone

If you decide to work with a stone, it's a good idea to cleanse it. Why? Because even if there's no negative energy attached to the stone, it probably contains some energies that you'd just as soon not cross over into your dream work. Any general stone cleansing will do. If you're in a hurry to get started, though, place the stone in the freezing compartment of your refrigerator, and say the chant below.

**Stone of Earth, receive this cold**
**Let it freeze out what is old**
**Ice, remove what I don't need**
**As I will, so mote it be**

In twenty-four hours, you'll have a clean, fresh tool to help you weave your dreams.

Following the cleansing, hold the stone in your dominant hand until you feel it begin to pulsate. Then lift it to your third eye and visualize a white light surrounding it. Say:

**Stone of Earth, be Stone of Dreams**
**Bring the visions that I deem**
**Aid in change and memory**
**As I will, so mote it be**

## The Dream-weaving Process

Now that the stone is cleansed and programmed, you're ready to begin. But how does all this dream-weaving stuff work? In short, you decide what you want to dream about, go to sleep and dream the dream, then re-invent the dream to suit yourself during a later sleep session. That's all there is to it. Concerned that you might not be able to dream about specifics on command? Then ask Cerridwen for help (see Appendix IV for characteristics of each Goddess), and follow the steps below.

# ❖ Dream-weaving Exercise

1. When you retire for the evening, decide what area of your life you want to dream about. This could be your financial situation, your love life, your career, or any other life aspect that you would like to change.

2. Before you drift off to sleep, hold the stone in your dominant hand and state your dream intentions. Then place the dream stone under your pillow and say the following chant to Cerridwen.

> **Cerridwen, Shifter of Shapes and of Life**
> **Stir this dream in Your cauldron tonight**
> **Show me in detail what I must see**
> **To make positive changes in my reality**

Close your eyes and go to sleep.

3. The next morning, review your dream step by step. Look carefully for areas that necessitate change, and pay close attention to any problems that cropped up during the dream. Some folks like to write their dreams in a notebook. This makes it easier to recall specifics during the reinvention process. Think about how you could rewrite the dream "script" to make your reality a better place to live.

4. That night, replay the dream in your mind, but change the script for a better outcome. Repeat step two, but change the chant to the following:

> **Cerridwen, Shifter of Shapes and of Life**
> **Stir this dream in Your cauldron tonight**
> **Shape it, mold it, build it well**
> **So that, in reality, it starts to gel**

5. Repeat steps three and four as needed—that is, until you achieve your goal.

Five steps: that's all there is to it. When one part of your life tapestry is woven to your satisfaction, simply move on to the next. And before you know it, your life will become the happy, rewarding, and comfortable place that you always knew it could be.

# The Ultimate Wisdom

The ultimate wisdom is something our mothers taught us as children, but we seldom practice. That something is, of course, good manners. Well-polished manners open doors. They aid in business success. They even help us form friendships, relationships, and partnerships. No doubt about it. They provide one of the most valuable tools necessary for mundane living. But what do they have to do with spirituality, the Crone, and menopause? Everything!

Just like the other folks in our lives, deities appreciate good manners. Archetypal or not, they like hearing "please" and enjoy helping those who say "thank you." They like being consulted and definitely appreciate being looked up to. I've never known one to turn a deaf ear on someone whose tongue dripped with effusive praise.

The point is, if you want the Crone to help you and work Her magic for you, you have to give Her some special treatment.

A good place to start is daily prayer. This practice serves several purposes. It is a daily reminder that, no matter what happens, your Crone is always listening and will always be there for you. Also, it puts the Crone on notice that you appreciate Her guidance and need Her help. But best of all, daily prayer guarantees that your Crone will send some special blessings your way, and one can never have too many of those.

Three daily prayers follow. You can use these or, if you like, you can write more personalized prayers of your own.

## Morning Prayer

Wisest Crone of many names
I thank You for this day
Walk with me and guide me as
I face what comes my way
Please lend Your strength and wisdom
As I strive to do my best
To use this new beginning
To benefit myself and all the rest
Of humankind and Nature's own
And help me to understand
That how I live my life today
Affects the cosmic plan
Wisest Crone of many names
I thank You for this day
Please help me be the best I can
As I live and work and play

## Prayer for General Wisdom

Oh gracious Goddess, Lady Crone
Show me the wisdom You alone
Hold within Your fragile hand
Let me see it as I stand
Each day upon the Earth's sweet face
As I rush about and race
Through my day and do my work
Please let me see it where it lurks
In trees and rocks and flowers sweet

In plants and dogs and those I meet
And let me hear its message clear
This I ask You, Crone so dear

## Bedtime Prayer

Ancient Crone, protectress, friend
This day is finally at an end
Thank You for the gift of time
For moonlit nights and soft sunshine
And thank You, too, O ancient Crone
For wisdom gained from time alone
For days well spent and good deeds done
And laughter, tears, and just good fun
And all the things You've given me
But as I put my head to rest
I ask you, heed this one request
As I sleep, watch over me
And let my dreams come peacefully
Protect me from all harm and ill
Seen, unseen, imagined, real
And grant my life be free of sorrow
Should I wake to see tomorrow

Before we close this chapter, there's one more thing you should know. It's a tidbit I picked up during my personal transition. Menopausal wisdom gathering goes down easy and tastes sweet but, if you're not prepared for the flavor, the aftertaste can be rather bitter. This is because wisdom involves change, and change seldom enters our lives without wreaking some sort of havoc. It's important to remember that creation is born of chaos and that completion springs from the creation process. Coming to that understanding definitely curbs the aftertaste. But if it's still there, this last tidbit will relieve it entirely: Know that when the wisdom gathering is done, you'll be a brand new woman. You'll be the Goddess complete: the Goddess come full circle.

# Chapter 3

# Life is Just
# a Party

My first encounter with She-Who-Nags might have gone more smoothly if I'd just understood why She was there. But I didn't ask. I didn't care. All I knew was that Her appearance meant the end of life as I knew it, and I wanted Her to go away. It never occurred to me that my current life wasn't so grand, or that it could be improved upon. Sadly enough, my own stubbornness nearly cost me the fun-filled, exciting life I've come to love. I count myself lucky that She-Who-Nags was determined, tenacious, and blessed with a stubborn streak twice as wide as my own.

Although the duties of personal Crones vary, they each have one initial mission in common. It is, of course, to personally deliver an invitation. Not just any old invitation. It's a very special one addressed only to an elite group of women: those who've paid their dues and deserve a reward.

She-Who-Nags, like Her counterparts, was only trying to do Her job: open the gateway for my new life, and offer me the chance to become everything I'd ever wanted to be. In short, She'd entered my life to give me a ticket for a cosmic make over—an opportunity to metamorphosize from the mother role into a graceful, beautiful, and powerful creature. I'd just been too stubborn to accept. So She had to get my attention. The hard way.

When I finally welcomed my Crone and accepted Her wondrous invitation, life took on new perspective. For the very first time, I began to see youth for what it really was. Difficult. Mind-boggling. A series of starts and stops on the road of life with lots of hand-slaps in between. It was nothing more than a learning period designed to teach me how to behave, how to respond, and how to achieve. To put it bluntly, it was only a dress rehearsal for the beginning of life.

At that discovery, I really got excited. I suddenly realized that menopause could bring me exactly what I longed for: a chance to put all the lessons of youth to use. I would have the opportunity to apply them and reap their benefits without worry of disapproval. After all, I wasn't some half-baked teenager anymore. I was a perfectly well-done grown person, complete with all the trimmings.

At last I could say what was on my mind, freely and completely. I could discuss my feelings openly and honestly, and share my most intimate thoughts with others. I no longer had to worry about conforming to society or its pressures. Why? Because after reaching thirty-five, I realized that age didn't matter much any more. I was a participant in the mid-age ranks—one of those women who the young view as senile and the elderly see as impudent. There was nothing left to prove to anyone but myself. It was the perfect place to be in life, and I loved it.

Once the Crone offered the luxury of societal nonconformity, other freedoms presented themselves, too. For example, I didn't have to cater to the general sense and standard of the feminine. I didn't have to look like a fashion doll, worry if I had a bad hair day, or spend an hour every morning coating my face with makeup. I was at liberty to love my body as it was and let its inner beauty—the beauty I was born with—shine through. Gone were the days of miserable shoes, uncomfortable clothes, and boring work. At last, I could work where

I wanted, spend time on projects that were close to my heart, and apply my talents in the areas they were most needed. The weight of the world seemed to jump right off my shoulders and out of my life. It was a wonderful feeling. I'd never felt so relaxed, so necessary, or so total.

Menopause, like puberty, is a rite of passage, and its transition is as individualized as the person it affects. Some women find it difficult and perplexing. Others see it for what it is: a chance to change their personal reality and redesign their lives.

How you view the transition and experience is strictly up to you. It can be wonderful or awful, celebratory or unnerving. It's all in your perspective. One thing's for sure, though. If you go into it with a closed mind, you'll miss the best time of your life.

## Sass: The Great Attitude Adjuster

Viewing menopause as a celebratory event isn't difficult. All it takes is a new attitude. So what's wrong with the one you have? Nothing. You're already a positive thinker. You obviously believe in yourself and in the Crone. You know what that combined power can do for you, and you've embraced it fully. But to manage this transition smoothly and enjoy it as it was meant to be, you need something more. Something you probably haven't thought about in years. What you need is a hefty dose of sass!

Sass is a powerful magic that adds spunk to an otherwise dull existence. Never mind that your mother taught you it was synonymous with impudence. When it comes to menopause, it's the one ingredient that can literally change your whole frame of mind. Even better, it can save your sanity.

The fact is, age makes us feel more reserved. It encourages a more conservative view of life. We joke less. We play less. Suddenly, acting like a lady is the right thing to do. And there's nothing wrong with that. We're beautiful, elegant creatures. We're full grown women.

But when was the last time you giggled? Flirted with someone for the sheer fun of it? Or did something silly because you wanted to? If it's been too long, a sassy attitude is in order. For one thing, it keeps life from being the same old stale routine. But its most potent magic lies elsewhere. It constantly reminds you that you're special and there's more to you than the elegant, full grown woman. Sass revives that vibrant, sexy, desirable part of you. It calls out the fun you that's always been there but somehow got misplaced along the way.

It's hard to jump into sass headlong, especially if you haven't used it in a while. It needs exercise, development, and careful nurturing. More importantly, you need the confidence to use it again. Start out slowly. Before you know it, life will regain its fun and you'll feel empowered enough to take on anything, even the physical symptoms of menopause. The suggestions below will get you started.

## Affirmations

Daily affirmations play an important role in keeping sass fresh and new. Stand in front of a mirror and look yourself in the eye, then say your affirmations. Don't have a clue what to say? You can begin by practicing the ones I've provided. Then write your own to better suit your personal needs. Here are three practice affirmations:

**I am vital, vibrant, and sexy
I am the feminine force**

**I am Beauty personified
I am Woman**

**I am perfect in my strength and power
I am Goddess**

The key to successful affirmations is to believe what you're saying with every ounce of your being. Once you believe it, it manifests in reality. And once it manifests, there's no stopping the sassy new you.

## Smile

Make a conscious effort to smile frequently. It will lift your spirits, lighten your mood, and make you feel good about yourself all day. Besides, others will wonder what you're up to!

## Laugh

If something's funny, laugh—not to yourself, but right out loud. Laughter is a powerful magic all its own. It breaks tension, eases depression, and diffuses undesirable situations. Because it's contagious, it can also change the negative, serious moods of those around you into something lighthearted and positive.

## Play

It's especially important during this transition to take time out to play. Can't remember how? Not to worry. You used to play as a child, so the process isn't totally foreign to you. Start out slowly. Go to a park and sit in the swing. Rock back and forth, then give yourself a good hard push. If that's a little much for you, play in the privacy of your own home. Try a set of crayons and a coloring book. It doesn't matter *how* you play, as long as you *do*.

## Be Friendly

My mother used to say that you could catch more flies with honey than you could with vinegar. She was right. People always respond more positively to a friendly approach than they do to a sullen one. Besides, it's another one of the great contagions. If you're friendly, others will respond in kind. Give it a whirl. It lifts the spirits and also imparts an unbelievable boost of physical energy.

## Flirt

Women, by nature, are born flirts. Somewhere between childbirth and menopause, though, we carefully pack our flirtations away so we can get on with the business of serious living. We just don't think we need them anymore. Wrong! One casual flirtation can do more for the ego than all the "atta-girls" in the world. If you have trouble with flirting, practice on your lover. In lieu of that, try a store cashier or someone in a public place. Don't do something outrageous or anything that might get you in trouble. Be subtle. The bat of an eyelash, a wink, or a direct look are good ways to start. Remember, the keyword here is "casual," so less is better. You're not looking for a long-term relationship. You're only learning how to be sassy.

## Wishes, Niches, and Dreams Come True

Menopause is just a heavily disguised party. It has to be. Otherwise, everyone on the planet would want a ticket. Its disguise is a little like a cocoon. The wrappings are dull, drab, and tough—sometimes even a bit scary. But if you wait long enough, you get to see true beauty and power emerge. And that's when the magical festivities begin.

Magical festivities? You bet. Menopause provides us with the most powerful magical period in life. If we wish it, it can happen. If we want it, we can have it. It doesn't matter how far out of reach our goals appear, if we desire them strongly enough, they can materialize right out of thin air. It's the only time in life we can make all our dreams come true. Sound hokey? It's not.

Fact is, most women don't even find their niche in life until they reach menopause. It's not because their niche isn't there. It's because they're so busy trying to meet everyone else's expectations, they just don't have the time to meet their own.

Take me, for instance. I'd always dreamed of being a writer but, when it came time to enroll in college, my parents convinced me to major in pre-med. They said I could starve to death before I ever got published or saw my first advance check. And even though I didn't want to admit it, I knew they were right. So, I went through college taking courses that were foreign to me. I studied hard and did well. I was accepted into medical school. But even after all my hard work, it didn't work out. Sadly enough, I discovered I was an empath and that the medical profession just wasn't for me.

Not to be deterred, I pulled myself up by my bootstraps and went through life trying this and that. Over the years, I tried my hand at playing the stay-at-home wife and mother, the legal secretary, the office manager. I went back to school and became a licensed manicurist. None of it worked out for me, though. None of it filled that empty spot inside. No matter what I did, I felt like a robot just going through the motions. And when I got tired of it, I decided to change my reality. I zipped off an article to a well-known publication, and the rest is history. After all, here you are, reading this book.

The point is, you've probably spent a lot of time doing what others thought you should do and being who others thought you should be. Don't think of it as wasted time, though. It gave you some very valuable tools. Experience. Insight. Determination. Now it's time to dust them off and put them to good use. With their help, you can do what you've always wanted, and be who you were born to be. Will it be easy? Probably not. Will it take work? Undeniably. But don't shy away or put your dreams on the back burner again. Just this once, take a chance. Reach for your dreams. The rewards will definitely be worth the effort.

## ❖ The Find Your Niche Ritual

If you have trouble finding your unique place in life, or can't seem to muster the courage to focus on your dreams, this ritual will put you on the right track.

**Materials:**

> A container to symbolize your niche (use your imagination—
> a bird's nest, a seashell, or even a matchbox will do)

A small snippet of your fingernail or hair
Small quartz crystal
Powdered thyme
Vegetable oil
Orange candle
Yellow candle
Purple candle

Anoint the candles with oil, then roll them in powdered thyme.
Place the purple candle on the altar and light it. Say:

**I give myself to the universe**
**I dance joyfully to its rhyme and verse**
**I hear its music and its call**
**I accept its blessings—one and all**

Place the "niche" container in front of the candle and say:

**Here is my niche, my unique place**
**It's where I belong, my personal space**
**It holds the keys to who I am**
**And who I become in the cosmic plan**

Place the fingernail or lock of hair inside the niche and say:

**I place myself inside this niche**
**A token symbol of my wish**
**To find where I belong at last**
**In the cosmic plan, so wide and vast**

Place the orange candle to the right of the niche. Light it and say:

**I attract what's meant for me**
**As I will, so mote it be**

Place the yellow candle to the left of the niche. Light it and say:

**With success, this spell I bind**
**What I wish for shall be mine**

Close your eyes and hold the crystal to your forehead. Visualize finding your niche, the place that you fit. See yourself being happy and fulfilled. Then place the crystal in the niche and say:

**I place this stone of power last**
**And as I do, the spell is cast**

Let the candles burn down entirely, then put the niche in a spot where you'll see it every day. Know that the universe will place you exactly where you need to be.

# Your Dreams and Wishes

Now that the universe is at work searching for your unique place in life, let's talk about your personal dreams and wishes. We all have them. They're important to us. And once we reach the menopausal transition, with all of its inherent power and influence, these desires can manifest in reality quicker than we can say "so mote it be." This is one of the greatest gifts menopause has to offer. Used recklessly, though, it can also be one of the most dangerous.

During the early stages of my transition, I didn't have a clue. I went about my life as I always had. No one told me the truth about menopause—that it was more than hormonal change, that it involved an increase in power. No one told me that it involved an increase in magical ability. My lack of information wasn't just sad, it was tantamount to letting a child play with fire. And, like everything else in my life, I learned about it the hard way.

Soon after our move to Missouri, my husband and I invited some folks over for dinner. The meal was great, the conversation was animated, and a good time was had by all. Or so I thought. The next day, my husband phoned me from work. He was livid. Our dinner guests had told everyone they knew that we were Satanists. Apparently, they'd decided that an arrangement of decorative plates in our kitchen bore the shape of an inverted cross.

I wasn't just aggravated. I didn't just come unglued. I hit the ceiling. And when I peeled myself off, I remember thinking how much easier our lives would have been if those idiots had just fallen down the steps and broken their necks on the way out the door. But I didn't stop there. I went on to dream up an assortment of other punishments that I thought fit the crime. Of course, it never occurred to me that any of those angry thoughts could possibly manifest in reality. After all, I was just blowing off steam.

Fortunately for me, no one wound up with a broken neck. There were injuries, though, and they were my fault. What I didn't realize at the time, was that the increase in power and magical ability had heightened my capacity for wish manifestation. It also meant that I suddenly had the power to hex and heal in the bat of an eye. It scared me half to death.

Here's the bottom line. Menopause is so magically powerful that it often brings about something that I call "unconscious magic." This means that even without the normal spell props like incense, candles, incantations, etc., your unconscious magic can manifest and become reality. All it takes is a fleeting thought fueled by uncontrolled emotion. We don't even realize that magic is afoot, much less that a spell has been signed, sealed, and delivered.

Fortunately, there is a way to remedy the situation. All you have to do is take charge. Refuse to let emotional chaos control your thinking patterns. The best way to do this is to remove yourself, at least temporarily, from the volatile situation. Think about something else. If that fails, involve yourself in an unrelated activity. When you're calmer, look at the situation with an objective eye. Then decide how you can remedy the matter to the best benefit of all concerned. You'll be glad you did.

But what about real wishes? The things that we actively want, consciously hunger for, and constantly dream of? The heightened power of menopause brings them to quick fruition, too. With that in mind, it's a good idea to stay with structured spells when working with wishes. It will keep fleeting thoughts at bay and guarantee your success.

## Tips for Pursuing Your Personal Wishes

1. **Consider any personal wish carefully.** Is it really what you want? Will you be happy for a long time if it comes to fruition? How will the end result affect your life? The lives of those around you?

2. **Work out a strategy.** Be specific about what you want and how you want it to happen. Write it out step by step.

3. **Incorporate your strategy notes into the spell.** Use it as a set of instructions for the universal forces. Don't worry that you're being arrogant. The universe and the deities who reside there are literal forces. Left to their own devices, they always take the shortest route from point A to point B. How the end results affect others is not something they consider. Their only concern is that the requested results manifest in reality. The how, when, and what are your responsibility. Just think of the instructions as a map you might give to a friend, then use them. Doing so can save you tons of time, heartache, and Karmic trouble.

4. **Finally, expect results and prepare for them.** Remember, this is your time and your turn; whatever you want can be yours. All you have to do is ask for it!

## ❖ Generic Wish Spell

**Materials:**

Written wish manifestation instructions
Small quartz crystal

3 tablespoons powdered sage
3 tablespoons vegetable oil
Orange candle
Yellow candle
Purple candle
Fireproof dish filled with soil or sand

Anoint the candles with oil, then roll them in powdered sage. Place the purple candle on the altar and light it. Say:

**I call upon the universe (or your choice of deity)**
**I call upon its rhyme and verse**
**Hearken, hearken—hear my plea**
**Grant my wish—so mote it be**

State your wish to the universe, then read the set of manifestation instructions clearly, firmly, and with feeling. Place them in front of the purple candle.

Place the orange candle to the right of the paper. Light it and say:

**I attract this wish to me**
**As I will, so mote it be**

Place the yellow candle to the left of the paper. Light it and say:

**With success, this spell I bind**
**What I wish for shall be mine**

Close your eyes and hold the crystal to your forehead. Visualize your wish manifesting exactly as you've planned. Then place the crystal on top of the paper and say:

**I place this stone of power last**
**And as I do, the spell is cast**

Fold the paper nine times and light it with the purple candle. Place it in the fire proof dish to burn. Leave the crystal between the candles until they burn down entirely. Don't leave candles unattended. If your attention is going to be diverted, you may want to burn them in a fire-proof setting such as a bathtub or deep sink. Bury the ashes and the crystal either outside or in a potted plant.

# Eccentricities, Weirdness, and Fun

One of the neatest things about menopause is that it gives us an opportunity to truly reinvent our lives. It's more than finding out where we belong and getting an idea of what we should do with our existence. It gives us a chance to change the way we look at the business of day-to-day living, to handle things as we see fit, and gives us license to embrace our personal peculiarities and eccentricities. Menopause gives us permission to have fun.

My Aunt Myrtle was a gracious, lovely woman with flawless manners. No matter how annoying things were, she never showed her displeasure or voiced her true feelings. To do so would not only have shown a lack of breeding, but would have branded her forever as "unladylike." In the deep South, that was a fate worse than death.

After a few years of menopause, though, Aunt Myrtle unwittingly reinvented her life. It all started on a brisk spring day in her back yard. She was on the sun porch repotting her plants when she spied something from the corner of her eye. She peered into the yard just in time to see a young man jump her fence, shinny up the plum tree, and proceed to steal the fruit. Of course, she was furious. She grabbed up her broom and quietly crept outside. He never even noticed her until he was well into a good flogging. And by the time she knocked him out of the tree, he was only too happy to leap back over the fence with his life intact.

I drove up a few minutes later. Aunt Myrtle ranted and raved. She bucked and snorted. She pranced around like a little bantam rooster ready to battle his way into the hen house. I was so amused, I could hardly contain myself. Finally, when I could get a word in edgewise, I reminded her that such behavior was "common" and that Southern ladies didn't act that way. At that, her eyes twinkled with delight. She smiled a sweet, dimpled smile, looked directly into my eyes, and said, "Menopause is fun!" Then she burst into laughter.

Aunt Myrtle was right. Menopause *is* fun. If you're not convinced, look at some of the fun you can have with everyday activities. Take the grocery store, for instance. You can dash through the feminine protection aisle without a care in the world. No need to worry about whether you've got a decent supply of tampons in the bathroom cabinet. No need to worry about birth control sponges and foams. No need to worry about anything in that aisle. The best part of not having to worry? You just saved a bundle of money. This is fun!

You get up in the morning and notice that your hair looks a lot like the punk rocker's next door. No need to spend an hour trying to make it behave. Instead, you just tie it up smartly in a scarf or tuck it under a sassy hat. Then you gently explain to your daughter (the one with the beautifully coifed hair) that the pimple she's so concerned about won't last forever. After all, you don't have any (try not to giggle). This is fun, too.

It's the dead of winter, and everyone's shivering with cold. Your neighbors keep turning up the heat and adding fuel to the fireplace. Their utility bills skyrocket, and they know there must be some mistake. They shuffle through the snow to ask if your bill was extraordinarily high, too. Be kind and gentle when you tell them "no." Explain that you have no need for artificial heat. Your hot flashes keep you warm. Menopause is *really* fun!

The fun doesn't stop there. It touches every part of life. It has to. This is the Crone's transition, and She's the ultimate party animal. Remember the eccentricities and peculiarities I touched on earlier? Couple them with personal opinion and you really have a party starter. One of my great-great-great aunts was blessed with such a combination. A woman of many accomplishments, she saved an entire regiment of wounded Confederate soldiers from certain death at the hands of the Union army. She was the first Poet Laureate of Texas. And she was eccentric to the hilt.

Aunt Mary was in business for herself in a time when most people thought it held no place for women. One afternoon, she arranged a business meeting with a gentleman in the lobby of a local hotel. The man brought his girlfriend with him. This wouldn't have been so bad if the woman had just taken a seat and been quiet until the meeting was over. But such was not the case. Constantly interrupting the meeting, she asked this question and that. Since none of her questions had any sort of merit, it became increasingly obvious that the woman was vying for the man's attention, and had no intention of letting another female talk to him—for business or otherwise. She clearly suspected that Aunt Mary was trying to steal her fellow.

Now Aunt Mary had very little patience for ignorance, and even less for airheads. After nearly thirty minutes of this nonsense, she rose from her chair and stood directly facing the woman. Her voice rose loud and clear. "Sometimes it is better to keep one's mouth shut and be thought a fool," she said, "than to open it and remove all doubt. Now hush, woman, before I thrash you soundly!" Then with a wink, she seated herself again and resumed the meeting.

Great Aunt Betty, a turn-of-the-century town historian, used to start her morning with a daily exercise routine. Though that sounds normal enough, she didn't jog, jump rope, or aerobicize. Aunt Betty's morning ritual consisted of donning her husband's trousers and turning cartwheels all the way down Main Street. And when she was done, she simply meandered back through town as if nothing at all unusual had happened.

While I'm sure there were lots of whispers about her strange behavior, no one ever mentioned it to Aunt Betty. They didn't dare. After all, there was no telling what a cartwheeling woman in men's trousers might do if pressed!

The Crone's gift of eccentricity allows you to say whatever you think whenever you want. It gives you license to be outrageous, flamboyant, and even a little sarcastic. It entitles you to do as you like no matter how bold, brazen, or crazy it may seem to the outside world. No need to worry about what others might think. Your loved ones will just scratch their heads in wonder. The rest of society will blame it on the "change." And what do you care? Aren't you having fun?

Discovering eccentricity has brought me more joy than I can say. For one thing, I'm now at liberty to commune with Nature in a way I never could before. I carry on real conversations with plants, stones, and flowers. I talk out loud to the animals I work with. I even scream at the universe when I've had a bad day.

No one thinks much of it anymore. They just shrug their shoulders and tell their friends I'm menopausal. They have no idea that these oddities won't pass. They have no idea that this strange behavior is making me healthy.

Yes, it's true. Weirdness is actually good for your health. According to recent studies, a complete disregard for societal rules, combined with a good sense of humor and an unblocked flow of creativity, keep disease at bay. So, go ahead. Be weird. Have fun. Indulge your eccentricities. And if anybody has the audacity to ask what the hell is wrong with you, simply say it's part of your personal health regimen.

## Tossing Out Stress and Mess

No matter who you are, how old you are, or how you live your life, stress eventually creeps in and tries to ruin the party. It aggravates everyone, but coupled with hormone imbalance and physical changes, it can really take its toll. Granted, a sassy attitude and a few personal peculiarities go a long way toward relieving its pressures. But sometimes it takes more than that to ward it off. Sometimes it takes a different kind of attitude adjustment.

In order to deal with stress successfully, we have to change the way we look at anxiety-related situations. This means trading in the thinking patterns we've held dear for a lifetime for new strategies. It's not as difficult as it might seem. In fact, this is one area where we, as Crones, really shine. With all the major changes going on in our lives, we realize that one more adjustment won't make any difference. And once we get to that conclusion, we've nearly won the battle.

When it comes to relieving stress, most of us look toward the cause of a problem because it stands to reason that finding a solution will make it go away. Sometimes this works. But more often than not, it doesn't. Why? Because most of the time, situations that bring stress into our lives aren't totally of our own doing. And that being the case, we just can't fix them. At the end of it all, the stress is still there. The problem still exists. We are still there, too. The whole ordeal leaves us feeling empty and useless. It's a hopeless situation.

If, instead of dwelling on the problem, we looked toward our reasons for feeling stressed, we'd stand a much better chance of success. That's because our feelings (rather than the situation itself) are what make us anxious, tense, and nervous. Once we understand why we feel the way we do, we can work through these areas one at a time. The stress leaves. The problem no longer concerns us. It's a much better solution.

Another way to manage stress is to head it off at the pass. This keeps minor problems from snowballing into the anxiety attack from hell. Some practical strategies are listed below. Give them a shot. It may be the nicest thing you've ever done for yourself. For additional stress relief help, see Chapter 6.

## Stress Reduction Tips

1.  **If it's not going to matter to you in five years, don't worry about it.** Why? Because if it's not a long-term issue, it's not part of the big picture. This means it probably won't have much impact on your life. Besides, mental energy is a precious commodity, and there's no reason to waste it on something trivial or meaningless. Forget about it. Use your energy to handle more important issues.

2.  **If you can't fix it, let it go.** It's human nature to want to solve the world's problems. We worry and agonize, and constantly rack our brains for answers and solutions. While this is a grand gesture, we must finally realize that some things are simply out of our control. Solve what you can, and let the universe take care of the rest.

3.  **Remember that when someone is upset with you, they are the person with the problem.** This doesn't mean that they are wrong, or that you don't need to apologize. What it does mean is that something you said or did pushed their emotional buttons, hurt their feelings, and triggered an outburst of anger. All you need to do is take the time to talk about the problem. Apologize for your actions. Then forget about it.

4.  **Don't do guilt.** This is probably the most difficult strategy to follow because women have, for centuries, willingly carried the guilt of the world. We apologize for things that aren't our fault. We accept the blame when things go awry. Sometimes, we even find ourselves doing things we don't feel comfortable with because someone else expects us to. This is because we are, by nature, the world's peacemakers. Peace is a good thing, but accepting guilt to achieve it is personally damaging. For one thing, the peace is short-lived. Guilt takes over and, before we know it, misery sets in. For another, this sort of guilt acceptance breeds resentment. It

makes us angry with those we love and angry with ourselves. Fortunately, the key to removing guilt from our lives is simple. All we have to do is realize that what's done is done, we can't take it back, and make a mental note not to repeat that mistake.

5.  **When the going gets tough, implement a stress prevention chant.** Here's an example:

> **Atropos, Iris, Hecate, and**
> **All Ancient Ones, come take a stand**
> **Please grant a pleasant, happy day**
> **And hold all stress and mess at bay**
> **Crush it before it hits its mark**
> **And makes my world seem bleak and stark**
> **Then transform its gloomy energy**
> **Into power I can use effectively**
> **To handle whatever comes my way**
> **This, Ancient Ones, I ask today**

# Heating up the Party: Utilizing Hot Flash Energy

If you want to stir up a conversation between a group of menopausal women, just mention hot flashes and night sweats. No woman in the room hasn't had them. No woman in the room doesn't hate them. And every woman in the room will tell you that they top the list as the most aggravating side effects of the menopausal transition. After all, it's embarrassing to have sweat rolling off your nose in the dead of winter. It's disconcerting to wake up in the middle of the night because your pillow and sheets are wringing wet. Even worse, it just doesn't fit the picture of what we expect ourselves to be: the cool, calm, collected women who can handle anything.

Fortunately, there are some easy and inexpensive ways to remedy these problems. To relieve night sweats, keep a glass of water by the bed. A quick drink provides instant relief and puts you back on the way to peaceful sleep. It's easy to control hot flashes, too. Drink peppermint tea (one heaping teaspoon of dried peppermint leaves to one cup of boiling water). This works almost instantly and, when consumed daily, can also keep night sweats to a bare minimum.

As ridiculous as it may sound, you may not want to take any action to relieve these problems. Hot flashes and night sweats are actually good for you, and comprise some of the most valuable gifts the Crone has to offer. From a physical standpoint, they increase blood circulation and boost your metabolism. This means you'll burn calories faster and you won't have to worry about your feet going to sleep. There are other advantages, too. They relieve the bloating caused by water retention. They flush minor toxins from the body. And best of all, they reduce wrinkles by feeding natural moisture back into the skin.

From a spiritual standpoint, hot flashes and night sweats are even more valuable. As the heat rises in the body, personal energy gains momentum and rises, too. The need for productivity becomes nearly overpowering. This is why some women have trouble going back to sleep after waking up with night sweats. The same pattern is true of magical power. It fills the body with energy, opens the psyche, and if it's not harnessed for productive use and spellwork—poof!—it can seep out into the cosmos, wasted and unused.

Granted, it's a shame to waste this powerful, productive energy. But how do we use it to boost our magic, especially when it wakes us up in the middle of the night or surfaces during a busy work day? Try some of the tips below to get started. Later, other ideas will surface. Before you know it, you'll find your personalized ways to harness this power and how to use it for the most potent magic you've ever performed.

## Tips to Harness Productive Energy

1. **Keep a notepad handy.** Take a second or two to jot down any ideas that swirl through your brain. There will be lots of these, so just capture what you can. Often, entire spells are born of these mini-sessions. Don't worry if one idea seems unconnected to another. Some thoughts may simply relate to areas of your life that need change. Others may bring new perspective to some spell-work or spiritual growth you've been considering.

2. **Work knot magic.** All you need for this is a piece of cord; a foot or two will do. As you feel the heat rise in your body, tie a knot in the cord and say something like:

> **I tie up power in this knot**
> **To save its force and potency**
> **It's safe within this bit of cord**
> **Until the time I set it free**

   When there are nine knots in the cord, use it to boost magical work by untying the knots and unleashing their power. As you untie each knot, say:

> **Potent knot of endless power**
> **I give you life and set you free**
> **Bring me what I ask of you**
> **Boost this spellwork's energy**

3. **Meditate.** It's especially easy to focus during these periods, so you won't have to worry about idle thoughts upsetting your state of altered consciousness. Use the meditation sessions to talk to your Crone, gain new insight into your spiritual growth, and uncover any personal obstacles on your personal path.

4. **Wish.** This is a great idea for night sweat energy, especially if insomnia sets in. Focus on wishes, goals, and needs, then channel the energy toward the desired result. This magic is not only extremely powerful, it supplies the practitioner with a wonderful side effect. It uses energy so quickly that afterward, you'll be too tired to do anything but sleep.

Of course, it's perfectly fine to perform "formal" spellwork during hot flashes or night sweats, too. Some of the most powerful Circles I've ever cast have been engineered with sweat dripping from my nose. If this appeals to you, try themes like healing or divination. The results will speak for themselves.

## Sex: Friend or Foe?

Sex. When associated with menopause, this tiny word probably evokes more questions, more emotion, and more worry than any other word in the English language. Part of the problem is what we read. Most articles on menopause speak of a decrease in sex drive, a lack of passion, and difficulty in reaching orgasm. The other part of the problem is that we're afraid that everything those journalists say might be true. We're afraid that we may never have great sex again. And if that's so, there's no point in having sex at all. As a result, we talk ourselves into a general lack of interest. We decide that we no longer need sex, we no longer want sex, and we'd be perfectly happy if no one ever wanted to have sex with us again.

This sort of attitude is not only ridiculous, it's detrimental to our emotional health. It makes us feel worthless and unattractive, tired and used up. As a result, we become depressed. After a while, we become angry, irritable, and miserable. All we want to do is plop down on the pity pot and sit there for the rest of our lives.

This is no way to start a party. If you're feeling like this—even a little bit—summon your sass, grab your new attitude, and wrap up in your newfound eccentricity. It's time to wage war on the Analyst again and, armed with these weapons, your victory is assured.

The first step toward winning the war is to look at the fun side of the menopausal sex issue. Remember those buttons and bumper stickers that read, "I'd rather be forty than pregnant"? I used to think those were pointless wastes of metal and paper, but now I see their wisdom. Forty is good. It's fun. It's exciting. And it's usually the time we're invited to the menopausal party. Of course, that brings many new things to life, but one of the best gifts it has to offer is worry-free sex. No more moon-blood. No more labor pains. No more aggravation. Just pure, raw, unadulterated sex, anytime you want!

Next, forget everything you've read about the sex/menopause issue. Even better, don't read any more articles that draw an association between the two. Remember that some journalists don't research well, and those who do occasionally miss important data and information. More to the point, remember that just because an article appears in a well-known magazine doesn't make its contents infallibly true. No matter what the journalists say, know that you can make liars of them. Decide that you're the exception to the rule, and then take steps to make it happen.

But what about the lack of hormones and the physical changes that accompany menopause? Don't they have any effect on sex at all? They do, but only to a small degree. For the most part, these conditions affect a decrease in the body's natural vaginal lubricants. This is a problem that can be remedied in several ways, but the quickest fix is to use a water-soluble gel. If you prefer to use an herbal solution, try taking ten drops of motherwort[1] tincture on a daily basis (see tincture recipe, page 177).

Of course, all the artificial lubrication in the world won't help if you're just not in the mood. What then? First of all, there's nothing unusual about not wanting or needing as much sex as you used to. It doesn't mean you're frigid or that there's something wrong with you.

1. See footnotes, page 228.

Menopause is simply a different sort of period than the pubescent time of the Maiden and the childbearing years of the Mother. It's a time when we tend to explore our inner workings, discover our personal independence, and come into our own. We have more of a need to spend time alone, and less of a need to share the intimacy of sex with a partner. It's nothing more than that.

There are things you can do to put yourself in the mood for sex, though. The same stuff doesn't work for everyone, however, so go through the list and experiment with the ideas that seem appealing to you. Don't try anything that makes you the slightest bit uncomfortable. Doing that will only inhibit you and keep you from having the greatest sex you've ever had.

## Tips for Getting Sexy

1. **Masturbate.** A good number of women, especially those who began their sex lives early, have no idea what really turns them on. Why? Usually it's because their partner took control of sex early on, leaving little time for personal experimentation. Masturbation is a great way to find out what feels good and what doesn't. Once you know what you like, share it with your partner. You'll find you're in the mood more often if you know your needs will be met, too.

2. **Experiment with another woman.** Many sex therapists insist that lesbian encounters can do wonders for the sex life. This is because women have less of a tendency to rush during sex. They take it slow and easy, and automatically allow time for sexual stimulation and arousal.

3. **Make time for foreplay.** If you prefer male partners, train your lover to take his time. It takes women (especially menopausal

ones) longer to reach orgasm than it does men, so they may need some extra time and attention. Make sure your partner understands that the whole body is an erogenous zone, and that foreplay should not start and stop with the breast and genital areas. Necks, ears, toes, and elbows can be very sexy, too.

4. **Fantasize.** It's okay to pretend that you're having sex with someone other than your partner. Pick someone dashing and exciting. If money and power turn you on, try a celebrity. If the adventuresome type does it for you, try a biker, an outlaw, or someone with a military background. It's your fantasy—your secret—and you can choose anyone you want.

5. **Pretend you're the leading lady in a porno movie.** Playing a role disentangles you from your emotions and relieves inhibitions that keep you from having fun. Best of all, it relieves nervous tension and allows you to experiment freely with new ideas and satisfy personal urges. This can make you feel extremely sexy.

6. **Lessen the frequency.** When sex is an everyday affair, it starts to feel routine. And routine is just that. It's boring. Make your sexual encounters a special event. Instead of having sex every day or so, take a few days off. Taking a break increases desire and passion. It may be all you need to put you back in the mood.

Never toss sex aside just because you've entered the Crone stage. Not only is it fun, it's very therapeutic. For one thing, it's good for the blood circulation, and that means a healthier body. It's also a great tension-reliever. Sex before bedtime can stop insomnia in its tracks, and it practically guarantees a good night's rest. Most importantly, though, those who go to sleep stress-free and satisfied will wake up that way, too. A healthy sex life is the perfect prescription for a positive attitude and general happiness.

Here's one more thing for you to think about. There is no sexier creature on the face of this Earth than the menopausal woman. She wears her experience as casually as her favorite sweater. It shows in her walk, her talk, and the way she handles her life. She exudes confidence, elegance, and intelligence, and she is beauty personified.

Know that you are this woman. You hold all these qualities in the palm of your hand. If doubt creeps in, just remember that you are the Goddess come full circle. You are the Goddess complete. And there's nothing sexier than that.

## ❖ Great Sex Spell

Once in a while, everyone comes to a point where they feel that something is missing from their sex life. If you want to add a little oomph to yours, try this spell. These four easy steps are guaranteed to chase away the doldrums, bringing excitement and passion to new heights!

### Step 1

A few hours before your encounter, anoint some red votive candles (the number isn't important) with vegetable oil and sprinkle some powdered cloves on them. As you light the candles, say:

**As fire ignites these wicks to flame**
**Desire flows freely through our veins**

### Step 2

Next, you'll need to prepare a passion drink. If you perform this spell in the spring or summer, use the recipe for cherried wine. If you perform this spell during the fall or winter, you may want to prepare hot buttered rum. Both recipes follow.

## Cherried Wine

1 jar of maraschino cherries
1 bottle of fruity-tasting wine

If you're not sure what sort of wine to buy, try blush zinfandel or reisling. If you prefer a non-alcoholic beverage, it's perfectly fine to substitute apple juice with a little cinnamon and clove for the wine. Pour the wine into a glass container and add the cherries and juice. Blend the mixture well with a spoon.

## Hot Buttered Rum

1 quart apple juice
¼ cup dark molasses
1 stick butter (not margarine)
Cinnamon sticks
1 ounce rum for each mug

Combine juice, molasses, and butter in a glass pot. Stirring constantly, heat on low until the butter melts. Pour one ounce of rum into a large mug, then fill with juice mixture. Stir with a cinnamon stick and serve. If you prefer a non-alcoholic drink, just leave out the rum. It's still a great drink, and omitting the alcohol won't diminish its magical power.

# Step 3

Finally, as you stir the magical mixture (the rum is stirred on the stove, the fruity wine in a glass container), chant something like:

**Fruit so sweet and rich with fire**
**I conjure you—bring back desire**
**I stir you up, and with you, passion**
**Excitement flows through every ration**
**Mix well the juices of desire**
**Bring back to sex its missing fire**

If you are using wine, you should now cover the container with plastic wrap and chill for several hours. If you are using hot buttered rum, serve it hot.

## Step 4
When the time comes, pour up the passion drink and serve. Prepare for the time of your life!

# Completion versus Perfection

Goddess complete or not, all menopausal women seem to have one thing in common. They think that Croning means personal perfection. Of course, this causes all sorts of trouble. The fact is, no one is perfect, not even the deities. Take Athena, for instance. She once lost Her cool at a spinning contest. The result of Her hissy fit? Arachne, Her opponent, lived the rest of Her immortality spinning webs and walking around on eight legs. Bacchus, outraged that anyone would dare to cross His path, swore that He'd feed the next trespasser to His lions. The victim was a girl named Amethyst. Fortunately, Diana interceded and turned Amethyst to stone to prevent her from becoming lion snacks. Pandora couldn't stay Her curiosity, Achilles had his heel, and Zeus had lots of trouble remaining faithful to Hera. The only thing perfect about any of these deities is the awful mess they made of the situations at hand.

The truth is, attending the Crone's party does not offer us total perfection. It does, however, give us the power to deal with our shortcomings and see them for what they are: interesting challenges that season our lives. It makes us realize that errors in judgment don't constitute the end of the world, and that the only people who don't make mistakes are those who aren't really living. More important, it makes us realize that it's perfectly normal to screw up now and then, and that there's no reason to beat ourselves up when we do. After all, if the deities we look up to and count on are flawed, it's ridiculous to think that we, mere mortals, might somehow come out unblemished.

What the Crone's party does offer is completion. It means that we've successfully lived the Maiden's life and learned about fun, and play, and love. It means that we've successfully lived the Mother's life, given away our moon-blood, and picked up important nurturing, nesting, and organizational skills along the way. It means that we've graduated, and it's time for advancement to the top of the Goddess theocracy—Cronehood—a place where we can put everything we've learned to use. At long last, we're allowed to hang onto the precious power of our moon-blood, keep it inside, and use it exclusively for our own personal regeneration and revitalization. And that's a good reason to celebrate.

# Chapter 4

# Mirror, Mirror
# on the Wall

Beauty. It's the one thing that we, as women, seem to worry the most about losing. Why? Because over the years, we've learned that it opens doors, helps us get what we want, and makes life easier. One of the most powerful machines in the female toolbox, beauty forces others to take notice and gives us an opening to state our opinions. While the thought of losing this tool is devastating, the thought of losing it to age is even more so.

The Analyst understands that the beauty issue is our point of least resistance, so She plans Her heftiest attack at its base. It's a smart move because She knows that how we feel about our physical appearance often colors the way we see ourselves in other areas. And if She can win this battle, She's already won the war.

The fact is that no one is every really satisfied with the way they look. It doesn't matter that the human race is an assorted bunch with members in all shapes, sizes, and colors. We've somehow managed to come up with the idea that beauty takes on a particular form—a form that, in its narrowness, does not include our race as a whole, but singles out only a few members as being truly beautiful. So we go through life worrying about crow's feet, extra pounds, and double chins. We concern ourselves with graying hair, cellulite, and wrinkles. Even worse, we've come to believe that the outer image is somehow indicative of our personal worth as human beings. Since most people don't even come close to meeting the "beauty standard," perhaps it's time to end that line of thinking and give some thought to how we came to that conclusion in the first place. The answer is simple. The Analyst has an army. We call it the media.

Every day we pass thousands of billboards sporting men with rock-hard abs and women with silicone breasts. Magazine ad campaigns lead us to believe that we can look just like the folks pictured if we use a particular kind of makeup, wear a certain brand of clothing, or shave our bodies with a special type of razor. Television commercials are just as bad. They implore us to dye our hair, whiten our teeth, and stay fit by working out on machines that were obviously invented by the Marquis de Sade. Perhaps the most powerful mind-benders, though, are the cartoons we let our children watch. Every super hero/ine depicted looks like Ken or Barbie.

Think about it. When was the last time you saw an ad centered around someone short and fat who wasn't contrasted with someone tall and thin in an effort to sell the latest diet plan craze? When was the last time you saw a television commercial whose main character really looked like your grandmother? How many times have you seen an animated cartoon hero or heroine whose body wasn't lean and whose waist wasn't whittled down to near nothingness? Don't worry if you can't remember. Those spots were probably never even filmed.

After the media gets our attention, the Analyst goes to work. She does Her best to convince us that we must be lithe, busty, tanned, and slim to be worthwhile and, before long, we begin to believe that it's not good enough to be a real person. We believe that anything less than media beauty is somehow lacking in intrinsic value. So we struggle to fit in. In desperation, we try everything possible to emulate the images created by some Hollywood ad executive. And when we fail miserably, our ego crumbles like some old dust clod under a broom, leaving us to feel inadequate, worthless, and ugly. Round one to the Analyst.

The point is that it's time to stop being puppets, whose actions and thoughts are dictated by the media, and take a good look at what beauty really is. What makes people attractive is their individuality and uniqueness. Most of our outer appearance comes from the gene pool of our parents and ancestors, and there's not much we can do about it.

Maybe what we really need is a changed mindset and a fresh perspective on outward appearance. So what if you carry a few extra pounds? All that means is that you have a higher gravitational pull than some folks. What does it matter if muscle bulges refuse to form on your frame? It doesn't. The fact is, you won't ever need to have your clothes custom-tailored.

This is not to say that you shouldn't strive to eat right and keep your body in good health. All I'm suggesting is that you learn to love your body as it is, and make friends with it. Once you begin to see its good points, you'll stop concentrating so hard on what's wrong with it. You'll be a much happier person, and I guarantee the new mindset will radiate outward.

## Making Friends with Your Body

Even if you've always thought of your body as public enemy number one, you can beat the Analyst at Her own game. Think about everything your body does for you. It houses the organs that keep you alive and vital. It takes you where you want to go. It tells you when you need nourishment, and reminds you not to overdo it by warning you before real pain sets in. In short, the body is your protector.

If someone had dedicated their entire life to your protection and bent over backward serving you, wouldn't you at least be nice to them? Maybe even like them a little? The truth is that you wouldn't give a hoot what they looked like or care a whit about their minor flaws. You would love them just the way they are. Such is the case with your body.

# ❖ Body Befriending Ritual

Start by making a two-column list. In the first column, write down all the things your body does for you. In the second, list all the things you do for it. If your body comes up on the short end of the stick, don't worry. It's never too late to make amends, for your body is not only your protector and friend, it's an extension of you.

Now that you realize your relationship with the body is one-sided, it's time to do something nice for it. Fill the bathtub with warm water. Add some bubble bath or oil in your favorite scent. A shower will work, too, but a long soak in the tub is much more luxurious. Light a pink or ivory candle and your favorite incense, and turn out the overhead light.

Undress and slowly sink down into the water. Inhale the aroma and watch the flicker of the candle against the bathroom walls. Close your eyes, and spend a few moments just soaking and reveling in the relaxation of your body. Stretch your legs and your arms. Wiggle your toes and fingers. Roll your neck from side to side. Feel the warmth of the water soothe the tension in your muscles.

When you feel completely relaxed, open your eyes. Lovingly and sensuously lather every part of your body—a bath sponge works well for this—paying careful attention to each nook, cranny, and curve. As you wash, visualize each part of your physical body being cleansed of any feature that you find disagreeable. Rinse them away with lots of water and slowly pat yourself dry.

After the bath, smooth on body lotion or cream. Apply it liberally and slowly work it into your skin as if you were massaging a lover. Feel your skin drink in every drop of moisture and grow soft and silky under your fingers.

By now, all the tension has left your body and you should be feeling very pampered. Take a deep breath and exhale fully. Remember that you are the image of your creator. Close your eyes and say:

### I am Goddess!

Repeat this affirmation until your mind is thoroughly convinced. Then, remembering that you are Goddess, face a full-length mirror and look at yourself. View the line of every curve and angle with new perspective. Trace them with your hands. Look at your body from each side. This is the body of a Goddess. There is no imperfection.

More than likely, the Analyst will creep in about this time and laugh at you. Push Her from your mind. If She refuses to go, yell at Her. Ordering the Analyst to leave not only empowers you, it lets Her know She's losing ground.

Face the mirror again and wrap your arms about yourself, hugging your body. Say:

### Body, you are perfect
### In every single way
### I'll love you just the way you are
### Forever and a day

Repeat this exercise at least once a week or whenever you begin to feel self-conscious about the way your body looks. After a while, you'll be such good friends with your body that the Analyst and Her army won't have any effect on you.

## Dressing for the Cosmic Party:
## Utilizing Color and Personal Style

No matter how much we learn to appreciate our bodies, something strange happens when we reach the Crone stage. Most of us start pretending that we no longer feel the need to impress anyone. We act as if we've lost the need to turn heads, receive personal appearance compliments, or win the appreciative smile that once warmed our hearts.

Of course, it's not true. We simply stop trying to *make* an impression because we think that we can't. We think we're too old now, that we're past our prime, and that we just can't look as good anymore. What malarkey!

All women feel better when they think they look good. It's just the nature of the female. The menopausal transition doesn't take that away. In fact, it gives us an edge that younger women don't have. We can get away with wearing clothes that we never could before. And we can get away with it beautifully.

Dressing Crone-style is fun, hip, and fashionable. But best of all, it's comfortable. It allows us to do away with the clothing that fits like a second skin. The stuff that looks great but disintegrates if we dare to take a single breath or gain a half-ounce of water weight. It allows us to wear elegant, flowing outfits in fabrics that drape and move. They not only *feel* sensuous but look that way, too.

So, what should you wear? Whatever you look best in, which depends a lot on your body frame and sense of style. My sister, for example, has a small frame. She looks smashing in flowing cottons trimmed with eyelet and Battenburg laces. I, on the other hand, have a larger frame and broad shoulders. The more classic, tailored clothes in silks, wools, and linens suit me better. For casual wear, though, almost everyone can wear denim.

Only you will know what makes you feel good and look good, so experiment. Be daring. Let your imagination run wild. And don't forget to accessorize. Jewelry, scarves, belts, and hats not only make the outfit, they go a long way toward lifting your spirits.

But what about color? Does Crone dressing mean that you're reduced to wearing black, purple, and navy blue? Absolutely not. Although these colors are definitely Croney, they just touch the tip of the iceberg.

For the most part, Crone colors are bright, vibrant, and flashy. Their shades closely resemble the flash of fire found in well-cut gems and semi-precious stones. Crone colors are rich jewel tones. Here's how they size up magically:

## Magical Associations for Color

- **Black onyx.** Want others to stop meddling? Black onyx discourages folks from making you the object of gossip, well-meaning interference, and encroaching on your privacy. Wear it when you need to get to the bottom line, search for discrepancies, or need an extra dose of wisdom. Use it, too, to call on your Crone.

- **Aquamarine** (pale blue). Try this shade when stress levels are high, when you feel out of sorts, or when the anxiety attack from hell looms near. It tends to clear away confusion and fill the void with nothing but peaceful, calming energy. It's also a great color to wear when you're ill, for the energy it emits is physically as well as emotionally healing.

- **Turquoise** (blue green). If you're a workaholic or need to get your priorities straight, this shade is good medicine. It forces you to take a step back, look at things objectively, and put things in the proper perspective. It's also great for knowledge retention.

- **Sapphire** (dark blue). This color is a terrific organizational tool. Its energies aid in clearing out, straightening up, and making way for the new. Wear it whenever you feel structure is lacking in your home, your business, your family, or your life.

- **Smoky topaz** (brown). If you're feeling scattered and can't seem to get your thoughts together, try this shade. Its earthy, stabilizing energy lends itself to issues involving common sense and clarity. It also works well to diffuse uncomfortable situations, and aids in good decision-making.

- **Peridot** (yellow green). Peridot is a sassy, lighthearted color that quickly transfers its joyful energies to all who wear it. It clears away all remnants of anxiety, depression, and feelings of worthlessness. Wearing it will not only bring your smile back, it will lend you the energy to grab all the gusto life has to offer.

- **Emerald** (dark green). If you lack confidence, ambition, or a sense of independence, this shade is for you. It gives you a feeling of power and makes short work of life's challenges and obstacles. Wear it, too, when your endeavors lack fertile ground or when you're short of cash.

- **Garnet** (deep red). Garnet is the ultimate power color. It's especially helpful when you have trouble taking charge, voicing your opinions, or exercising your authority. Wear it in the bedroom, too. Red lingerie has a tendency to increase sexual desire and passion, and allows you to toss aside any inhibitions that get in the way of your sexual fulfillment.

- **Ruby** (rose). When you're down in the dumps and feeling useless, run to your closet and find something in this shade. It's a great pick-me-up, and works wonders in the personal value and self-love department. It's also a great catalyst if you're in the market for some good old-fashioned romance!

- **Amethyst** (medium purple). Amethyst is the great relaxer. It eases chaos, activates the intellect, and keeps high-level stress at bay. It does have one side effect, though. Wearing it stimulates inner beauty and forces it to the surface, so be prepared to feel gorgeous all over.

- **Sugilite** (deep purple). If you feel like you're just one more body lost in a sea of anonymity, wear sugilite. Another power color, it demands respect and forces others to take notice. It's also a great shade for any endeavors dealing with spirituality, psychic ability, and magical power.

- **Golden topaz** (yellow). If you're out of ideas and at your wit's end, give this shade a whirl. It inspires, excites, and titillates the imagination into productive action. It also works wonders in the communications department by forcing others to pay attention to your views, your opinions and, of course, your newfound ideas.

- **Citrine** (yellow orange). Got the blahs? The prime motivator, citrine, picks up where golden topaz leaves off. Wear it for efficient time management, renewed productivity, and positive reactions to new projects. It's great for business endeavors, too.

- **Moonstone** (white, cream, ecru). Moonstone is the supreme cure-all. You should always keep lots of these colors in your closet. Used to accessorize (collars, cuffs, and trims) or complement (blouses, blazers, etc.), it magnifies the properties of the predominant color scheme. Need a super pick-me-up? Wrap yourself in it from head to toe!

Although the colors listed have specific magical properties, you don't have to wait for problems to surface before you wear them. You don't have to limit your wardrobe solely to these shades, either. Part of the beauty of the Crone stage is discovery. Try different shades and see what happens. Make notes of how individual colors make you feel, and the reactions they get from other people. Before you know it, you'll be dressing with the magical, powerful elegance of the Crone Herself—to say nothing of turning heads again!

## Reinventing Personal Beauty

Though the statement "Beauty is in the eye of the beholder" may be a quaint cliché, no truer words were ever spoken. We all have our own opinions of what's beautiful and what's not. Some people think dark skin is pretty, while others prefer light. Some folks like dark almond-shaped eyes. Others say that round light-colored eyes are more beautiful. Thin, willowy body frames are popular right now, but the Renaissance masters only painted women with a little meat on their bones. The list goes on and on, but one thing's for sure. Even after we make friends with our bodies, few of us ever take a look in the mirror and see true beauty.

So, who's responsible for our blindness? The media? Perhaps to a small degree. The Analyst? Somewhat. The fact of the matter is that we are to blame for the largest part of the problem. It's human nature to be critical of ourselves. And because we tend to concentrate on our physical imperfections, we seldom see ourselves as other folks do. We see the nose that's too long, the lips that aren't full enough, and the cellulite that creeps up the backs of our legs. We see wrinkles, sagging skin, and lackluster hair. We see all the things that other people don't.

If that's true, what do other people see that we can't? They see the sparkling smile, the twinkling eyes, and the elegance and grace of the feminine form. They see the joy of laughter, the wisdom of experience, and thrill of life yet to live. They see beauty that is obvious to everyone but ourselves: the total woman, the individual composite that makes each of us unique. Have doubts? Then try this exercise.

# ❖ The Facial Features Exercise

1. Take a picture of someone you think is beautiful. Look at their features separately (eyes, nose, mouth, etc.), as if they were the only thing in the picture. If you have trouble isolating the features, cut the picture apart. Go through each feature in this way.

2. Objectively evaluate each feature, asking yourself, "What's beautiful about it?" Probably nothing. More than likely, one eye is larger than the other, the eyebrow arches are uneven, and the lips are either too thin or too large. But don't stop there.

3. Examine the nose. Don't hurry. Take a good look. It's okay to laugh out loud. The perfect nose, not even the one surgically created, has never been placed on anyone's face. And separated from the rest of the face, all noses are just downright ugly!

The point is that physical beauty doesn't rely on any single feature. It's a complex combination of aspects that work together to complete the total picture. These aspects aren't all physical, though. They come from deep inside and are traits that you already possess, including self-confidence, a positive outlook, and spiritual awareness. Together, they form what is commonly known as inner radiance. It's this inner radiance that shapes the base for beauty and enhances the physical composite.

If you have trouble seeing your true beauty, the spell below is for you. It not only eases the personal criticism factor, but brings inner radiance to the surface.

## ❖ Inner Radiance Ritual

Take a glass of water and go outside on a clear, starry night. Look at the stars and study them for a moment. Take note of their beauty, their perfect clarity, and their differences. Notice how they are small, large, and even misshapen. Recognize that, like people, each individual star has a beauty all its own. After a few moments of contemplation, lift your arms to the sky and invoke the stars by saying:

> **Shining stars of brilliant light**
> **Beacons in the dark of night**
> **Light my way and help me see**
> **The true beauty within me**

Infuse the glass of water in your hands with star shine by saying:

> **Stars of brightness, stars of light**
> **Radiant jewels that shine at night**
> **Lend your power to this glass**
> **That I may shine like you at last**

Have a sip, then sit down and get comfortable. Think about your good qualities, the life you've experienced, and how much you've learned through the years. Think about your spiritual growth, the path you walk, and how you've begun to blossom as the Crone. Contemplate how that sets you apart from every other person on the planet, and how that makes you the beautiful, special person that you are. Then look up to the stars and say:

> **Twinkling stars in black of night**
> **Saturate me with your light**
> **Let your magic run its course**
> **And touch my spirit with your force**
> **Guide your radiance to my source**
> **And fill me 'til its glow springs forth**

Hold the glass skyward in a toast to the stars, and drink the infused water. Know that your inner radiance and unique beauty will surface and be apparent to everyone—even you.

# The Crone's Mark: Wear It with Pride

It doesn't matter how gorgeous the face is that smiles at us from the mirror, there are a few things that might keep us from smiling back in satisfaction. The few things in question are wrinkles: those tiny lines, furrows, crinkles, and creases that meander across our faces like highways on a road map. And no matter how prepared we think we are for them, their arrival usually scares the hell out of us.

The problem is that we're conditioned to think of wrinkles as an ugly part of the aging process. And that's simply not true. Like the creases on the palms of our hands, facial lines are powerful symbols. They represent every aspect of our life experience. They come from laughter and tears, smiles, worries, and deep thoughts. They represent who we were, where we went, and what we became as the result, for they form the road maps of our lives.

We need to understand that wrinkles are not punishments. Instead, they are the awards we earn from living: the prizes we earn from being, doing, and accomplishing. And we need to start looking at them that way.

At this point, you're probably thinking that if a wrinkled face is the trophy you get for winning the game, you'd just as soon not play. But before you make up your mind, consider this. In ancient times, the more lines one had on one's face, the more one was revered and valued. Why? Because they belonged only to the those who'd managed to survive the toughest of times, and lived to tell about it. They belonged only to the village teachers, historians, and wisdom-keepers:

those people who had accumulated the knowledge necessary for successful living and, in turn, could hand down their secrets to perpetuate tribal growth and life. It's little wonder they held the most valuable positions in the village.

Even though we live in a different time and place, maybe it's time we took a tip from those who lived before us and appreciated our time lines a little more. After all, we managed to sprout strong and sure in a fast-paced world. We learned to handle whatever life threw our way, and grew in the process. Then somehow, even in the chaos of life's everyday trials and tribulations, we survived to bud as individuals and blossom into beautiful, vital women.

The tiny marks we see in our mirrors every day are important, for they prove that we are forces to be reckoned with. They remind the world that we are powerful enough to conquer our problems, tenacious enough to achieve our goals, and wise enough to survive the interim. They remind the world that we are the wisdom-keepers, the elders, the teachers. But more importantly, they remind us that we are valuable. We wear the Crone's mark, and we've been personally selected to do Her work.

For this reason, I no longer see the wrath of age when I look at the lines on my face. Instead, I see wise old friends with important messages. The crow's feet and cheek creases remind me that life is full of smiles, and that laughter and a good sense of humor is always the best medicine. The lines that cross my forehead speak, too. They remind me that fretting is a waste of time, and that most of the things we worry about don't amount to a row of pins. My favorite one, though, is the crease that rests right between my eyebrows. It reminds me that my abilities to focus, concentrate, and think are more valuable than any other gifts I have. They make me who I've become: a Crone.

## Water: The Ultimate Beauty Treatment

Learning to accept and appreciate the Crone's mark doesn't mean that we shouldn't take care of our skin. In fact, She-Who-Nags reminds me constantly that the feminine connective tissue should be soft and supple, and that mine often resembles coarse grain sandpaper. It still needs all the stuff it always did, including careful cleansing, gentle stimulation, and proper nourishment. Only now it needs something more: lots and lots of moisture.

The reason skin needs extra moisture during this transition is that the hormonal changes caused by menopause tend to dry it out. This is true even if you've always had oily skin. The result? Flaking, itching, and, in the cold of winter, painful chapping. Regular exfoliation, a weekly mask, and the daily use of a good moisturizer will help, but to really give skin the moisture it needs, you have to get back to basics. And that means drinking lots of water.

Water is not only the most inexpensive beauty secret in existence, it's also more powerful than anything you can buy over the counter. True enough, commercial moisturizers smooth the skin and enhance its appearance. The problem with these products is that, because they can't penetrate all three layers of skin, they only work on the surface. This results in a temporary fix. And as soon as you cleanse your face again, you're right back at square one.

Daily water consumption provides a more permanent solution. Here's why. The human body consists mostly of water, and constantly uses its supply to function properly. It lubricates the organs, joints, and mucous membranes, and keeps the blood flow regulated. It also keeps the skin soft, moist, and pliable, and gives it the flexibility necessary to keep the body moving and bending during our daily routines. Here's where the problem comes in.

If we don't replenish the water that the body uses, it loses the capacity to handle its workload. This means that the body has to prioritize. The brain still works. The heart still pumps. You can even wiggle your fingers and toes. But skin moisture (not being nearly as important as the other functions) quickly goes by the wayside.

Drinking eight to ten glasses of water every day is the only solution. This not only provides plenty of moisture to hydrate the skin from the inside out, it gives you the benefit of an additional beauty treatment. It allows the pores of the skin to open and close properly and, as they do, any excess moisture is forced to the surface. This quickly flushes away the start of any toxins or impurities that can cause skin problems, and blemishes become a thing of the past.

But what if you don't like water? You might be wondering: Won't the water contained in coffee or soda do the trick? No. The caffeine in these beverages often cancel out the healing effects of water. Even worse, they can cause just as much dehydration as not drinking any liquid at all.

If you don't like the taste of water, the problem may be your area water reservoir. Give bottled water a shot. Then, if you have trouble drinking the daily water allotment, try measuring it out at the beginning of each day. Put it in a plastic milk container and take it with you. When the jug is empty, you'll know your body has had all the water it needs to function properly and to build really beautiful skin.

## The Fun Stuff: Pampering Your Skin

While water can work wonders with any type of skin, menopausal skin needs something more. It needs a good dose of tender loving care. This means a regular skin care regimen. Don't groan. Just try the routine that She-Who-Nags laid out for me. It will make your skin look and feel great, and it only takes about ten or fifteen minutes each day. Everyone can spare that.

The following skin care treatment doesn't require anything special. Any over-the-counter beauty aids will do. However, if you'd like to prepare your own toners and moisturizers, recipes are provided in the *Making Your Own Potions and Lotions* section of this chapter (pages 123-126). Once you have the necessary products, proceed as follows:

1.  **Remove makeup.** If you wear makeup, whisk it away with a little mineral oil and a few cotton balls. Mineral oil is inexpensive and much less likely to clog your pores than any cleansing cream at the cosmetic counter. Even better, it removes every kind of make-up you can imagine, from foundation and lipstick to eyeshadow and mascara.

2.  **Cleanse.** Turn on the hot water and work up a good lather with your favorite beauty bar or facial scrub. To prevent skin from sagging, you should wash your face using tiny circular motions and working in a counterclockwise direction. Rinse well with hot water, and then lather your face again. Use cold water for the second rinse, then thoroughly pat your face dry.

3.  **Tone.** Apply a little toner (witch hazel works well) to your face with a cotton ball. Use the same tiny, circular, counterclockwise motions described for cleansing the face.

4.  **Moisturize.** This is especially important at night, because skin loses moisture while you sleep. Apply the moisturizer sparingly. A dab on your forehead, chin, and each cheek will do. Work the lotion into your skin using outward, sweeping motions, then tissue off any excess.

That's all there is to it. To keep skin in really good condition, though, try a weekly mask. I like the ones that are made of green clay because they quickly draw all impurities out of the skin. To boost the mask's drawing powers, add rosemary as described in the *Making Your Own Potions and Lotions* section. It's good for your skin and leaves you feeling refreshed all day.

Even with all this pampering, the unfortunate fact remains: no one feels beautiful *all* the time. This is perfectly normal; it's just a part of human nature. However, if the doldrums take over and persist for a week or longer, you might want to try the following spell. Its powerful magic won't just chase the blues away, it may actually change the face that smiles back at you from the mirror.

## ❖ The Facial Beauty Spell

**Materials:**

> Small piece of rose quartz or blue lace agate
> 6 rose or violet petals
> 1 bottle herbal vinegar toner (page 124)

Thoroughly cleanse your face, then look in the mirror and scrutinize the areas you see as flawed. Visualize your face shifting and changing until it's perfect in every way. Caress the problem areas with the stone and chant:

> **Stone of beauty and perfect love**
> **Erase each flaw now as I rub**
> **Bring perfect beauty here to me**
> **As I will, so mote it be**

Drop the stone in the bottle of toner. Hold the petals in your dominant hand and say:

> **Venus, hear me from aloft**
> **And take these petals, rich and soft**
> **Bless them with Your beauty rare**
> **And grant the face I wish so fair**

Rub the petals over the problem areas, then add them to the bottle. Cap the bottle tightly and give it six firm shakes every day for a week.

Now you can use it daily as a toner after washing your face. As you apply it, say:

**Imperfections, go away**
**Perfect beauty is mine today**

## Enhancement is Enchantment

I don't work in professions that require me to wear makeup on a regular basis. Some days I spend sitting behind a computer desk at home, writing. Other days, I work at the local animal shelter. My plants and fish don't care how I look. Neither do the dogs and cats at the shelter. As a result, the cosmetic bag that once held a central position on my bathroom counter now resides in a dark and dusty corner in the cabinet below.

That's not the only reason for its new living quarters. I thought that entering the Crone stage meant not having to impress anyone. I thought it meant that I no longer had to buy into society's expectations. After all, I'd paid my dues—I was free of society's trappings, and I was perfectly beautiful just the way I was.

I was right. But only partially.

I discovered my error when I was asked to do a photo shoot with Sadie, my dog, for the shelter. It was a big deal because the photos were to be enlarged to poster size and used as decorations for the fundraising event of the year. I was thrilled. I felt honored. I couldn't believe my good fortune. I took my black suit to the cleaners and made arrangements to have Sadie groomed.

The day of the shoot arrived. I scrubbed my face, put on my suit, and grabbed Sadie's leash from its hook by the door. True to form, She-Who-Nags paid one of Her untimely visits.

"Where the hell do you think you're going?" She snapped. Her eyebrow arched. Her lips pursed. She'd assumed Her old-maid school teacher stance.

"To a photo shoot, and You can't come. Go away, now. I don't have time for You today." I stomped through the house in search of Sadie.

"Are you crazy?" She look at me in disgust and blocked my path. "You know damned good and well you've never been photographed without makeup!"

"So what?!" I countered. "This is a first, and life is full of them. Besides, I'm beautiful. I'm empowered. I am the Crone!"

"Right on all counts," She said with a grin, "but you've forgotten the basics. *Enhancement is enchantment.*"

Her last three words echoed through my brain. She was right. Enhancement is one of the most basic magical principles. I use it when I spend time writing spells in rhyme. I use it when I add props like candles, stones, and herbs to my magical efforts. It is present in my focus, my concentration, and the power that I raise. Enhancement is not only the glue that holds my spells together, but it is the catalyst that sends them soaring into the universe. And now, I was missing a golden opportunity—an opportunity to work a special kind of magic for myself. It didn't take me long to rummage through the bathroom cabinet and dust off my makeup bag.

The results were stupendous and immediate. I turned heads everywhere I went. My boss, who'd never seen me wearing makeup, almost didn't recognize me. Even my dog paid more attention to me. I spent the rest of the day aglow with the magic, thrilled with life, and quite pleased with myself. And to make things even better, I saw enchantment everywhere I looked, from the acorns in the trees to the sparkle of mica in the pavement. I *was* the enchantment and it was a wonderful, powerful feeling.

Whether you wear makeup or not is up to you. You are a Crone either way. The point is that enhancing your natural beauty is not a sell-out. It's a magical act that can work wonders for your ego. It can make you feel vibrant again. It can allow your sass to resurface. More importantly, it's the only personal magic you can perform that only takes a matter of minutes from the initial step to the end result.

## Scent: The Magical Intensifier

Scent is more than a nice touch. It is to beauty what decorative icing is to cake. It makes people take notice, teases the palate, permeates the inner core, and creates a delectable aura of elegance. It's the rich, sweet embellishment that pulls beauty together, intensifying its magic.

Using perfume is also therapeutic. It lifts the spirits, chases away the blues, and makes us feel like getting out and doing things. It's fun. I find that to be true especially during the Crone phase. Why? Crones no longer have need of those light, do-nothing baby powder scents. We can afford to be flamboyant, daring, and risqué. We can afford to be bold. With the timidity and shyness of youth out of the picture, we can afford to make any statement we please.

Choosing a scent that suits your sense of style isn't difficult. You know what you like. The hardest part is finding one that smells good on you. Everyone's body chemistry is different, so what smells good in the bottle won't necessarily smell good on your wrists. And even if it does, it may not smell exactly like it did in the bottle. For this reason, it's a good idea to experiment before you buy. It can save you tons of money and aggravation in the long run.

Today's perfume market is versatile, trendy, and has something for everyone. Like a designer fragrance, but can't afford it? Try one of the great-smelling impostors. Often, these are a less concentrated, more cheaply packaged version of the exact perfume you're lusting after.

Looking for something that no one else will ever be able to find? Check with your local New Age, occult, or herbal shop. Not only are most happy to blend a scent that meets your specifications, they'll keep the recipe on file so you can purchase it any time you want. In lieu of that, try blending your own special scents. Recipes in the *Basic Perfumery* section of this chapter (page 119) will get you started.

## The Signature Fragrance

There's nothing wrong with changing scents to suit your mood, but once you find the perfect one, you may want to consider using it as your signature fragrance. A signature fragrance is a personal scent that you always wear; a fragrance that's as much your own as the way you sign your name. But what about smelling like everybody else? Doesn't that defeat the purpose? No need to worry. Just as perfume aromas differ from bottle to body, they also differ from person to person. It's that body chemistry thing again.

The signature fragrance holds a very potent magic all its own. It keeps you in the forefront and on the minds of everyone you meet. One wisp of air is all it takes to carry your scent long after you've left a room. It leaves a subtle reminder of your presence, your importance, and your impact on the lives of those around you. Unlike the forceful, unpredictable nature of other connection/attraction magics, the signature fragrance works its magic gently and thoroughly. Even better, it soothes everyone in its path.

The magic of the signature fragrance isn't restricted to a dab on your wrists, knees, or cleavage. It has endless possibilities. Place scented cotton balls in your stationery box and gift wrap holder. Bring your fragrance alive in linens and laundry by tossing a scented handkerchief in the dryer. Dab it on unscented candles and rub it on light bulbs. Don't forget the work place, either. A scented cotton ball or two in your desk drawers will gently remind others that the contents inside belong to you, and that swiping your favorite pen may not be such a good idea.

# The Basic Perfumery

The recipes below are comprised of basic essential oils.[2] Because individual tastes may vary, no specific proportions are listed.

## Citrus Scent

Lemon Balm
Lime
Orange Blossom or Neroli

## Floral Scent

Jasmine
Magnolia
Ylang ylang

## Spice Scent

Clove
Cinnamon
Vanilla

## Wood Scent

Patchouli
Nutmeg
Myrrh

Start by blending one drop of each oil together. Add drops until you have a blend you like. Keep track of how many drops of each oil are used, then write down the recipe and keep it in a safe place. That way, you'll be able to duplicate the fragrance time and time again.

2. See footnotes, page 228.

# Beauty Tips from She-Who-Nags

Being beautiful is one thing. Being drop-dead gorgeous is quite another. Though most people disagree, it has little to do with makeup or outer beauty. It comes from feeling good about the way you look. When you feel good about the way you look, you feel beautiful. And when you feel beautiful, drop-dead gorgeous is right around the corner. It's as simple as that.

The following tips come from She-Who-Nags and are designed to make you feel beautiful. Give them a whirl and see what happens. You'll be amazed at the change in your attitude, appearance, posture, and style. So will everyone else.

## General Body Beauty Tips

1. **Use a bath puff, brush, or loofah instead of a wash cloth.** These items not only stimulate and refresh, they remove dead skin cells. This promotes new cell growth and skin regeneration.

2. **Use vitamin E in your bath.** Break open two or three capsules and squeeze the liquid into your bath water. This softens skin and the antioxidant properties of this vitamin promote skin cell regeneration.

3. **Apply body lotion liberally after baths or showers.** Rub extra into elbows, heels, and other areas where dryness is a problem.

4. **Add salt and baking soda to your bath.** To soften your skin, add a handful of salt and a couple of tablespoons of baking soda to your bath water.

5. **Relieve the bloating of water retention.** Drink a glass of water mixed with a tablespoon of vinegar. This is a natural diuretic. It works quickly, usually relieving the problem within an hour.

## Facial Beauty Tips

1. **Remove dead skin and promote cell growth.** Apply a thin paste of baking soda and water to your face. Rub in for only a second or two, then rinse well with cold water.

2. **For a radiant glow, apply a light moisturizer before makeup.** This also allows smooth, even foundation coverage.

3. **"Open" the eyes by tweezing stray hairs.** Tweeze from the upper eyelid, then brush the eyebrows in an upward motion. Only tweeze hairs under the eyebrow. Tweezing above them tends to give the face an unnatural look of surprise. To control unruly eyebrows, rub a bit of petroleum jelly on a cosmetic brush before grooming them.

4. **Place cold cucumber slices on areas irritated by hair removal.** This relieves the swollen eyes or puffiness that can occur. In lieu of that, use cotton pads soaked in cold witch hazel.

5. **Petroleum jelly is great for lips.** Massage some into lips every night to smooth away dryness and prevent chapping.

## Tips for Beautiful Hands and Feet

1. **Strengthen weak or brittle nails.** Mix equal parts of olive oil and white iodine (available at your local pharmacy) in a clean nail polish bottle. Shaking well before each use, apply the mixture twice daily to clean, dry nails.

2. **Keep cuticles soft and pliable.** Push them back with a towel after every shower or bath, then rub a dab of petroleum jelly into each one. This also prevents hangnails.

3. **Once a week, treat your hands to a massage.** Warm some lotion in the microwave for five to ten seconds to use for this purpose. Try it on your feet, too. It feels good and it helps prevent dryness and chapping.

4. **File nails straight across.** Work from the edge to the center in both directions. Filing them into ovals or points causes weakness, splitting, and breakage.

5. **Remove calluses and rough spots from feet.** Walking barefoot in the sand is a great method. In lieu of that, use a pumice stone on a weekly basis. Afterward, moisturize feet well and slip into a soft pair of socks. Wear them to bed to seal in the moisture.

## Tips for Beautiful Hair

1. **Control dandruff or oily scalp.** Dip your hair in ice water for the final rinse after shampoo and conditioner. This also gives the hair extra body.

2. **Rid hair of excess oil.** Pack tissue or cotton between the rows of bristles in your hair brush. Brush thoroughly.

3. **Add luster to dull hair.** For hair lacking shine and luster, add two or three drops of rosemary oil to your hairbrush. Brush hair thoroughly to evenly distribute the oil.

4. **Reconstruct dry or overprocessed hair.** Work a tablespoon of warm mayonnaise into freshly washed hair. Leave it on for three minutes, then shampoo thoroughly. It's a great reconstructor.

5. **Prevent hair breakage and split ends.** Use a comb instead of a brush on your wet hair. To untangle snarled hair, comb through the ends first, and then work your way slowly toward the roots.

6. **Trim your hair every month.** For quick growth, schedule the trim on the New or Waxing Moon.

7. **Get plenty of sleep.** Even if you don't feel the need to try any of the other ideas listed above, please add this last tip to your daily routine. It's not only important, it's imperative. You won't feel beautiful if you're tired, and you won't look that way either. Lack of sleep causes bloodshot eyes, black circles, and bags large enough to hold the family belongings. More importantly, you won't have the energy to become the magic—the enchantment—the powerful creature you were meant to be.

## Making Your Own Potions and Lotions

Sometimes it can be fun to make your own beauty aids, not to mention powerful. It's a Croney thing to do, and it's a great way to infuse your beauty aids with the desired magical qualities. The first thing to do is decide on a Goddess suitable for each recipe, depending on your idea of the beauty aid's purpose (see Appendix IV for guidance on this). Once you've called on your Goddess, begin the recipe. Add chants or affirmations as you mix and stir to give each beauty treatment its own personal magic. If you like, you can create an entire ritual around one recipe. The possibilities are endless.

Some of my favorite recipes are listed below. Magic aside, they're simple to make and you'll have the satisfaction of knowing exactly what you're putting on your skin. That luxury is not always available when you buy beauty treatments over the counter.

### Crone Soap

2–3 bars unscented soap  
1 tablespoon powdered cinnamon  
3 tablespoon dried rosemary  
1 tablespoon dried lavender  
1 tablespoon salt  
3 cups water

Use a cheese grater to grate the soap into a measuring cup, firmly packing it until you have a full cup. Place the herbs, salt, and water in a glass pot and bring the mixture to a rolling boil. Cover the pot, remove it from the heat, and let it stand for three to five minutes. Pour the soap into the herbal mixture, and stir well until the soap dissolves. If the mixture is thicker than you'd like, add hot water in small amounts until it's to your liking. Let cool, bottle, and label.

### Oatmeal Baking Soda Scrub

1 tablespoon uncooked oatmeal
1/2 teaspoon baking soda
1 large jar apricot facial scrub

Add the oatmeal and baking soda to the jar of apricot scrub. Mix well with a wooden spoon. Put a dab in your hand, add a little water, and work up a good lather before cleansing the face.

### Herbal Vinegar Toner

1/2 cup dried rose petals
1/2 cup dried chamomile
Peel of one orange
1 quart vinegar
Quart jar with a screw top lid
5 drops essential oil of your choice (optional)

Combine the rose petals and chamomile and place them in the jar. Using a glass pot, bring the vinegar to a full, rolling boil. Pour the vinegar into the jar and cap tightly. Shake the jar well every day. When the herbs lose their color, strain them out; then add a cup of water and the oil (optional) to the liquid. Leave the jar in a dark place for a week. A kitchen cabinet works well. Strain again to remove any sediment. Apply to clean dry skin with a cotton ball.

## Witch Hazel Toner

1 bottle witch hazel
2 tablespoons dried lavender
1 tablespoon dried chamomile[3]
1 teaspoon dried rosemary

Place all ingredients in the blender and mix on high speed for one minute. Pour the mixture back into the bottle and refrigerate. Apply to the cleansed skin with a cotton ball. Leave on two minutes, then rinse with cool water.

## Herbal Moisturizer

$1/2$ ounce beeswax
$1/2$ ounce coconut oil
$1/2$ ounce jojoba oil
$1/2$ ounce vitamin E oil
2 ounce sweet almond oil[4]
6 tablespoons dried comfrey[5]
3 tablespoons dried lavender
4 tablespoons dried rosemary

Place the herbs in a resealable plastic bag and shake well to mix. Lay the bag on a flat surface and press out all excess air. Using a rolling pin or a glass, apply pressure back and forth across the bag to bruise the herbs. For best results, continue the rolling motion for thirty to sixty seconds. Set the bag aside. Combine the sweet almond and vitamin E oils, then warm them in a glass pot over low heat. Stirring constantly with a wooden spoon, add the beeswax a little at a time, then pour in the remaining oils. Add the herbs and stir continuously until the beeswax is melted. Remove from heat and allow to cool for ten minutes. Strain out the herbs. When the mixture is cool, pour into little jars with tight-fitting caps. Label and refrigerate.

3, 4, 5. See footnotes, page 229.

## Rosemary Tightening Mask

1 large jar of green clay mask
1 tablespoon dried rosemary

Combine the ingredients and stir well with a spoon. Apply the mask to the entire face except the eyes and lips. Allow to dry, then rinse thoroughly with cold water.

## Egg Yolk Mask

1 egg yolk, well beaten

Smooth the egg yolk on a well-scrubbed face and wait for it to dry. Please refrain from talking, smoking, or anything else that requires the use of facial muscles during the drying period. The idea is allow the mask full drawing power, and cracking it will impede its benefits. When the mask is dry, rinse your face with cold water.

# Chapter 5

# Whose Life
# Is This, Anyway?

I used to consider myself a take-charge kind of woman. Self-discipline was my mainstay, and I was in complete control of my body, myself, and everything that crossed my path. I ran four miles a day, lifted weights, and constantly opted for the ankle express instead of grabbing the car keys. Fat grams, calories, and carbohydrates were counted. Every single bite that went into my mouth was carefully logged in a notebook I kept on the kitchen table.

Stress, anxiety, and nervous tension maladies belonged to other folks. So did depression, tears, and anger. As far as I was concerned, they were a total waste of energy. I had other things to focus on— good things—and I simply refused to spend one minute on anything even remotely negative.

Those days are gone forever. Gram and calorie counting is a thing of the past; I now drink coffee, scarf down fast food with sinful zest, and limit exercise to a daily stroll with my dog. I yell, scream, and cry with ease. I've even discovered stress and know what it means to want to choke the life out of some idiot just for fun. Yet, my doctor says I'm the most physically and emotionally healthy patient he has. So, what happened? I learned what taking charge of my life really meant!

# Health for the Whole Self

Health, physical fitness, and a positive outlook are wonderful things. There's nothing wrong with avoiding stress, working out, or eating well. Truth be told, there wasn't anything wrong with my old life either, except that there just wasn't any time left over for fun.

I seldom went shopping because the area malls seemed to breed stress and negative energy. I didn't go out to dinner because the food wasn't "healthy" enough. I couldn't go play with my friends because I had to tone and shape my body. Hell, I couldn't even read a good book. By the time I got through with my daily fitness and stress-avoidance routines, all I wanted to do was fall into bed. I finally realized that my life was living me instead of the other way around.

Once I decided to live again, I put aside some time to practice daily meditation. These personal time blocks started out as a way of pampering myself and getting in touch with my needs. The luxury of peace and quiet didn't last long, though. She-Who-Nags dropped by with a message.

"This is a waste of time," She spat. "An effort in futility."

"Nobody asked you. Now go away! You're messing up my state of nirvana!"

"Nirvana, my ass," She cackled. "You wouldn't know nirvana if it slapped you in the face! How could you? You don't even know how to live!"

"What?!" I was flabbergasted. "What do you mean?"

"Before you can truly reclaim your life and live it to the fullest, you must heal."

Then She popped out, leaving me to ponder Her words. It wasn't long before I figured them out.

As children, our parents teach us not to dwell on any of the negative things that happen to us. To do so provides the energy necessary for negativity to grow, to swallow us up, and eventually to leave us wallowing in a pool of self-pity. In short, we learn that thinking about our hurts and injustices will turn us into people who no one wants to be around. So we go through life waving our hurt feelings aside, ignoring personal unfairness, and hoping that our injuries will just vanish into the ether. They won't.

Injuries have to heal, and time doesn't always do the trick. Dealing with each wound on an individual basis is the only effective solution for true healing. Naturally, this isn't any fun. We usually have to cut through layers and layers of spiritual bandaging to get to the root of the problem, and sometimes we reopen other wounds in the process. Finding unexpected wounds is depressing, irritating, and often heart-wrenching. Because stumbling over an old wound makes us feel vulnerable, we have a tendency to stop, rebandage, and just go on about our lives with the same old problems.

Our inability to continue the healing process really has little to do with human vulnerability. We already covered the injury with spiritual gauze, and those who are truly vulnerable seldom have the strength to protect themselves at all.

The real reason that we forgo proper healing is because the Analyst keeps getting in our way. She tells us that getting too close to an old injury or picking at an old wound will hurt. The human system is simply not set up to disregard such a warning. If we try to ignore Her and go forward, we wonder with each and every step how much pain will follow. Apprehension takes over, red flags go up and, before we know it, our nerves are raw. We freeze in place, too terrified to put the next foot forward.

So, with the Analyst scaring the life out of us, how do we ever heal? We change our perspective. We look at healing from a new angle. We make it something fun, fresh, and exciting. In doing that, we get the upper hand and keep the Analyst from doing any further damage.

# ❖ Emotional Well-being Ritual

Make a list of everyone who has ever hurt your feelings. Include those who have treated you unfairly. It's okay to add your current high priestess or Sister Alberta at the Catholic elementary school. If they hurt your feelings, they belong on the list. Don't worry about whether the incident in question is a minor one, or whether you might have deserved what happened. Don't analyze; just write.

Go through the list and find the one person who pissed you off most royally or caused you the most pain. If you can't remember, ask your personal Crone for assistance. She has a perfect memory. Recall that incident in its entirety, but view it as if you were watching an old movie. See every detail, right down to what you were wearing. Play and replay the scene in your mind until you have every part of the situation committed to memory.

Now sit down and write that person a letter. Remind them of what they did to you. Be angry. Tell them exactly what you think. Tell them what a rotten excuse for a human being they are, how they're not fit to eat with pigs, and how you'd cheerfully rip them limb from limb if given half a chance. A weak voice will probably creep in at this point to remind you that your mother is watching you from two thousand miles away. It adds that she taught you proper manners, is mortified at your behavior, and that she'll faint dead away if you continue with this course of action. Ignore it. It's just the Analyst trying for one last stand.

When you're done, fold it several times, and write "JERK" on the outside. Enclose the word in a circle. Draw a diagonal line through it.

Set the letter ablaze in a fireproof container. Draw a large "X" through the name on your list. As the letter burns, play the offending episode through your mind one more time. Remember to view it as an old movie. Pick out any valuable information (lessons learned, experience gained, etc.) that could come in handy later in life, and jot it

down. Then visualize putting the movie back in its film can and tossing the container in the trash.

Take a deep breath and exhale slowly. Stretch your arms and legs.
Feel the power well up inside you. Stand with your legs apart and
your arms outstretched. Feel the universe surrounding you. Say loud-
ly and with feeling:

> **Mine is power**
> **Mine is health**
> **Mine is strength**
> **And emotional wealth**
> **I control**
> **My life and soul**
> **I am Goddess!**
> **I am Crone!**

Smile. If you feel like laughing, go ahead. It's a sign that your life is
on its way back to you. Laugh hard. Laugh loud. Laugh from your
very core. Laughter gives you power, and also signals your personal
Crone that you are ready for emotional healing. Invite Her to help you
by saying something like:

> **Crone of power, wisest Friend**
> **Come to my aid and help me mend**
> **Lend Your strength and lend Your power**
> **Increase my courage by minute and hour**
> **Stay with me through this ordeal**
> **O Crone of power, help me heal**

Do the healing ritual described above at least once each week, and
add names to the list as you go. Performing this rite quickly steals the
Analyst's power. Eventually, Her energy flow will ebb to the point
where you won't even be able to hear Her.

# Mental House Cleaning

Now that you're on the road to recovery, you need some time to get to know your Crone, Spirit, and self a little better. Say you don't have a minute to spare? Think again. The time is there somewhere. It's just well-hidden. Granted, finding extra time isn't always easy. You have lots of things to do and remember, so your mind is constantly in a state of clutter. Mental house cleaning takes time, and keeping the Analyst at bay takes energy. After a busy day, you just don't have much of either. So, how do you resolve the problem and still keep your life together?

The answer is to simplify. Begin by keeping a list of every task you complete at home and how much time you spend on each. Keep the list for a week and don't fudge. Write down everything, even if you don't think it's important. After a week, go through the list to see how you spend your time. Chances are you're overworked, underpaid, and didn't spend any time at all doing something fun.

Now go through the list again, this time day by day, and look for time-consuming areas. Think about how important those particular duties are to your life, and why you spend so much time on them. Is it because they really demand that much attention, or is it because the Analyst expects perfection?

The Analyst is easily dealt with. You are only one person, and you can't be everything to everybody. No one expects you to handle every task flawlessly. If you suspect the Analyst of wasting your time, just say "No!" Have a good laugh and make Her the object of your laughter. The Analyst hates that. She'll rush off in search of someone who might take Her more seriously.

## Finding Free Time

But what if fulfilling your responsibilities really does take an inordinate amount of time? The best way to handle them quickly is to tackle them from a fresh perspective. Here are some tips to get you started.

1. **If it's not important, don't do it.** For example, you don't have to clean house every day. A few dust bunnies never hurt anyone. Your family won't shrivel up and blow away if their clothes aren't perfectly pressed each morning. And who cares if dinner isn't served precisely at six? No, I'm not saying to let things go completely or indefinitely. I'm only suggesting that certain things be handled on a weekly basis rather than a daily one. If any items on your list fit that category, highlight them with a marking pen; then schedule one day each week when you can handle all of them.

2. **Learn to do things quickly without skimping on efficiency.** For instance, thirty-minute meals can be just as nutritious as those that take hours to prepare. Use the microwave or, even better, the crockpot. When you gather the laundry, use a dirty T-shirt to wipe the sinks and counters, then head for the washer. Toss house clutter into a large box and put everything away when the house is tidy. Instead of driving all over town searching for something you need, phone ahead to see if it's in stock.

3. **Delegate.** If you see an idle body, give it a job. Children, spouses, significant others, and roommates can wash dishes, sweep floors, and use the feather duster. Often, they can even mow the grass and do the shopping. Let them know it's a new day; from now on, they can pick up after themselves and be responsible for their own belongings. Write a name by any job that someone else can do for you.

4. **Organize.** Make a list and take it with you when you shop. Put things where you can find them, and put them away as soon as you're through with them. Lay out the next day's clothes and dole out lunch money before you go to bed at night. Let school books and briefcases sleep by the front door. If the meteorologist is calling for rain, leave umbrellas and galoshes there, too.

5.  **Get rid of unnecessary items.** Have a yard sale or box up every-
    thing you don't need and take it to the nearest rescue mission. A
    decrease in belongings means less to clean, dust, and fix. Besides,
    someone out there really needs that stuff. By making it available to
    them, you've done everybody concerned a good turn.

6.  **Don't worry.** Worry is, perhaps, the most time-consuming task
    we assume in this life. It's also the most ridiculous. No amount of
    worry in the world is going to fix a problem; only a sound solu-
    tion will. If you can't fix it, force it from your mind. You'll be sur-
    prised how much time you have left for fun.

## ❖ "Making Time" Exercise

Your goal in this exercise is to find a *minimum* of five free hours in
your week (preferably up to ten free hours) to spend on yourself. Use
the above list as a basis. Think of ways you might save time and what
arrangements will have to made in order to do so, then implement
your plan.

If you come up with less than five hours, reassess your situation.
The problem is probably leftover guilt supplied by the Analyst. Wave
it away. You owe this to your new self. Keep working with the problem areas until you can clear at least five hours of free time.

## Getting Rid of Excess Baggage

Now that you have some extra time, find a quiet place to examine the
things that clutter your mind. First, sort through any items that relate
to family, work, or finances. Look at each item carefully and decide
whether it's within your power to fix it. Make a note of any solutions
that come to mind, then take action and resolve those problems now.

Other issues might take more time to handle. Pack those away neatly in a distant corner of your mind with a promise to go through them again next week. However, most mind clutter consists of things we cannot change, repair, or rectify. If you find that to be true of your clutter, scoop it up, throw it in the nearest mental trash can, and forget about it. Hanging onto such garbage only feeds the Analyst, scares the Spirit Self, and exasperates the personal Crone.

Next, sort through issues relating to friends, foes, and acquaintances. Are there people in your life who make you crazy? Don't treat you well? Zap what little energy you have left? Take a good hard look at each of them. If they fall into any of the following four categories, then they fit the "energy bandit" genre and you need to toss them out of your life.

1.  **Users.** Never able to accomplish anything on their own, users beg for your assistance. Giving them a rundown of your busy schedule doesn't deter them; the fact that you have deadlines goes right over their heads. They plead ignorance and insist they don't have a clue as to how to begin the project in question. Then they appeal to your sense of values and friendship by remarking how grateful they'd be if you'd just come by and show them how to start. Finally, you agree, but once you arrive, they either disappear entirely or climb into the nearest easy chair to supervise while you sweat to their tune. They don't want your help or expertise. They want you to do their work.

2.  **Energy Suckers.** These folks usually ingratiate themselves to you, so it's hard to disentangle yourself from their lives. They're lovable and helpful, and always manage to be a good listener. So, what's not to like? From the second they grace you with their presence, they proceed to zap your energy. Fatigue sets in. At the end of a normal conversation, you're so exhausted that all you can think about is crawling into bed.

3. **Guilt Freaks.** No matter how busy or pressed for time you are, these people always have an agenda much more important than yours. While these folks might sound like the stereotypical "user," their tactic is much more harmful. Not only do they apply hefty doses of guilt when you refuse to stop in the middle of your project to come to their aid, they find fault with you when their endeavors don't work out as planned. Either you didn't help them in time, didn't follow their instructions to the letter, or were so concerned about your own agenda that your mind wasn't on the business at hand. No matter which way you turn, an unfavorable outcome is always your fault.

4. **Energy Bandits.** Energy bandits depend solely on others for their energy supply. They feed the Analyst and suffocate your spiritual growth, so if any of them live in your personal world, take every possible step to remove them. When they call, don't have time to talk. If they show up at the front door, be on your way out. And whatever you do, don't invite them over. If you don't feed their appetites, chances are they'll get the idea and fade out of your life.

It may take stronger measures than being assertive to rid yourself of these types of people. In that case, try the following ritual. It's incredibly effective.

# ❖ Bandit Banishing Ritual

**Materials:**

> 1 purple candle anointed with vegetable oil and
>   rolled in powdered lavender
> 1 tree leaf for each bandit
> Patchouli oil
> Pen
> Scissors

Take the ingredients to a spot where you won't be disturbed. Light the candle. Place the leaves, pen, and patchouli oil in the center of the area. Then, using the scissors as a wand and traveling deosil (clockwise), cast a triple Circle around them. On the first pass, say:

**My Crone protects me from all ill**
**Seen and unseen, quick and still**

On the second:

**I am empowered by my Crone**
**I have the strength to stand alone**

And on the third:

**I am free of chains that bind**
**My Crone cuts through them like thin twine**

Sit in the center of the Circle and close your eyes. Visualize the bandits standing in front of you and see the cosmic cords that connect you to them. Take the scissors and cut through a visualized cord. Say:

**(Name of bandit), of you I am free**
**Our cord is cut, and you must flee**
**I've started life over, it's fresh and new**
**There's no place in it now for you**

Then write the person's name on a leaf and draw an "X" through it with patchouli oil. Repeat the process with each bandit. When all the leaves have been named and anointed, place the leaves in front of the candle. Hold the scissors in your dominant hand and dissolve the Circle, traveling widdershins (counterclockwise). Say:

**Gone now all the stress and strife**
**And mess you've caused within my life**
**Gone, too, your power over me**
**By earth, sun, wind, and shining sea**

Let the candle burn out (under supervision). Take the leaves and toss them on the winds, saying:

**In peace and love, your leaves fall free
Gone forever from my personal tree**

## Pampering Yourself

When was the last time you felt truly pampered? If you're like most women, you probably can't remember. That's because as women, we are naturally the world's givers, nurturers, and care providers. Besides, we're taught as little girls that pampering ourselves instead of others is not just inappropriate, it's a sure sign that we're self-centered, selfish, egotistical human beings. Thus, we spend our lives tending to everyone's needs and concerns—everyone's, that is, but our own. So, when is it our turn? Sadly enough, the answer could be "Never!"—unless we break the rules and pamper ourselves.

I remember well the first time I broke those rules. It happened during a time when I'd just come out of a bad relationship and really needed to feel good about myself. I tried everything I could think of to make a new start. I reorganized my life, changed jobs, and found a new place to live. No matter what I did, though, that empty spot was still there. It seemed that the real me was lost somewhere, and I just couldn't find her again.

Finally, I realized what was wrong. I didn't have anyone to tend to my needs. There was no shoulder for me to cry on. No one to commiserate with. Not a single soul available to help pick up the pieces. Everyone I knew was involved in the business of living their own lives, and they just didn't have time to help me get on with mine. All I needed was a little pampering, and I was furious that no one saw fit to give me some.

That did it! I was going to be pampered that very day, and I didn't care what rules had to be broken. I ran to the kitchen and yanked the coffee maker's cord from the wall. A few minutes later, the appliance was installed in the bedroom within arm's reach of the bed. A mug rack, some antique cups, and a basket of gourmet coffees completed the ensemble.

For me, a coffeeholic to the core, this was pampering at its best. Every morning, the automatic timer started my coffee fifteen minutes before the alarm went off, and I leisurely sipped the rich hot stuff in bed. It was a wonderful feeling. Even better, it was fun!

That one little change opened a whole new world to me. I started thinking about who I was, what I wanted, and how I felt. As new likes and dislikes surfaced, I realized that my outlook on life had changed. I wasn't the same person I'd been five years before, one year before, or even last month. More important, though, I discovered that I was a uniquely important strand in the cosmic web, and that I held a very special place in life that no one else could fill. A tiny bit of self-pampering had turned into something I hadn't dreamed possible. It was the best spiritual therapy I'd ever had.

Spiritual therapy? You bet. Pampering yourself is equivalent to self-appreciation. And because you and the Crone are one, anything special you do for yourself, you also do for Her. Looking at it from that light, treating yourself well takes on a new note. Instead of being the root of all selfishness, self-appreciation becomes empowering and magical. Practiced often, it's the most sacred ritual you can perform.

Pampering yourself during menopause is important for several reasons. For one thing, you can't always depend on others to do the job. Even if you could, would you really want to? Other people have their own lives and their own agendas. They have their own priorities, and when they finish juggling their to-do lists, they're exhausted. The fact is, you could wait a lifetime and never get what you need.

Just for a moment, let's pretend that someone is more than willing to pamper us and has the time to do it properly. What would we tell them we need? Most of us have no idea. We've spent so many years tending to everyone else that we've forgotten what makes us feel good. We don't know what we like and don't like anymore. Before we can communicate our needs to someone else, we have to rediscover them for ourselves.

No matter how you slice it, no one can pamper you as well as you can pamper yourself. This is especially true during menopause. Because it's a totally transitional phase, our needs change just as our bodies do; that is, what feels good one day may not the next. The best thing to do is explore and experiment. Find out what makes you feel special, then take action. The end result? You and your personal Crone will bond in a way you never imagined possible. You'll also discover, as I did, that you're much more important than you thought. That the role you play in this life is unique. That no one can replace you. And that your value in the cosmic web increases every day.

## ❖ Self-appreciation Rituals

Self-appreciation rituals don't have to be expensive. In fact, treatments that cost little or nothing are often the most gratifying. Some of my favorite treatments are listed below as suggestions. Try a few and get started today. You'll be glad you did.

- **Rent that movie you've wanted to see.** It's the one that no one else in your household wants to watch. Put on your most comfortable clothes, gather a supply of your favorite beverages and munchables, and head for the bedroom. Pop in the movie, fluff your pillows, and get into bed. Enjoy.

- **Allow time for a daily nap.** In lieu of that, sleep late one weekend morning. Tell family members that lightning will strike them if they wake you.

- **Turn off the telephone ringer and slip into a comfortable spot with a juicy novel.** Don't stop reading until you've gotten through at least two chapters.

- **Keep a supply of incense and scented candles in the bathroom.** Fill the tub with your favorite bubblebath, light a candle and some incense, then turn off the lights. Soak until the water starts to cool.

- **Hire someone to clean your house at least once a month.** As long as they're there, make a point to have them do all the jobs you hate—things like toilet scrubbing, bed changing, window washing, etc. Remember, if you have it done on Friday, you won't have to spend any of your weekend time picking up stray clutter!

- **Make an appointment to get your hair cut.** Don't stick with your old hairstyle. Try something new. While you're there, check into the other beauty treatments they offer. Manicures, pedicures, and facials are generally inexpensive pampering rites.

- **Add some culture to your life.** Give yourself tickets to the opera or ballet. If your taste is less classical, get tickets to the concert of your favorite recording artist.

Other ideas might include shopping for new clothes, taking yourself out for dinner, or spending a day in the comfort of your pajamas. Use your imagination. You know what you want. You know what you need. In this case, what you do is not important. All that matters is that you learn to appreciate yourself, and that you start today.

But what if family members grumble about the amount of time you're suddenly spending on yourself? What if they try to make you feel guilty? Don't worry about it. It's just that wily Analyst at work again. If you're capable of ignoring all the mumbles, whines, and grumbles, then by all means do it. If not, reassure your family that you still love them, but you must have a little time for yourself. Then, as soon as you're able, sing this little ditty to the Analyst. It'll leave her quaking in her boots.

### "Analyst Go Away" Song

Sing this song to the tune of "Tah-rah-rah boom-de-ay" any time the Analyst tries to get the best of you. It's powerful medicine against Her manipulative antics.

**Tah-rah-rah boom-de-ay**
**Analyst go away**
**Run far away from here**
**My Crone is hov'ring near**
**She'll make short work of You**
**And kick You black and blue**
**If you keep bothering me**
**Go now! Just flee!**

# Reclaiming Your Home

Many years ago, the home belonged to the woman. She nested there, put things where she wanted them, and decorated to suit her personal tastes. She allowed man to brag that the home was his castle, but deep down inside, she knew better. After all, it was her touch that transformed the ordinary house into something really special—a comfortable place where family members could kick back, relax, and leave the rest of the world behind. In short, she created a sanctuary.

Today's world is much different. Nesting isn't high on our priorities lists. Many of us work outside the home, so we don't spend a lot of time there anymore. And those of us who do spend most of it scurrying around trying to get ready for the next day. We meet each other coming and going, each family member with a separate agenda. And when we finally wind down enough to take some time to kick back and just "be," we discover that we have no real nest to relax in. There's no real spot to call our own. No place that's exclusively ours. Not a single, solitary inch of house that calls our name.

That's why it's important to reclaim your home. You are the woman and the home truly belongs to you. Don't worry that your favorite feminist might call you a wuss. Even if you meet her in person, she never has to know. Don't worry that your mother will think you're selfish. So what if she lives across the street? You're a grown person. Besides, she can't see you right now. Just do it. Take action today. It's not only your inherent right as a woman, it's your job.

## Planting Your Claim

Start by planting some rosemary. According to ancient grimoires, this herb traditionally belongs to women. Its growth by the front door tells the universe that the home belongs to the woman who lives there. It sends out signals that, even though she allows others to share her home, she is the manager, the administrator, the have-all and be-all. As an added bonus, it also protects the home against the potential claims of others. No home should be without it.

## ❖ Rosemary Ritual

If you have a flower bed by the front door or can dig one, choose a spot as close to the threshold as possible. Otherwise, find a large clay pot for the task. Bless the flower bed or pot on the New Moon by saying something like this:

> **Blessed be this sacred Earth**
> **This breeding ground of love and mirth**
> **This partner in reclaiming home**
> **For myself and for my Crone**

Plant the rosemary when the Moon begins to wax. While it's fun to grow herbs from seed, try to find three plants for this ritual instead. By some fluke, almost all rosemary seeds are sterile. This means that even though they may come up, the sprouts are fragile and likely to die out before they really take hold. The plants, however, are hardy and spread easily.

Name the plants "Crone," "Spirit," and "Self," then bless each one as you plant it by saying something like:

> **In the names of Spirit, Self, and Crone**
> **I urge you now to grow**
> **Dig deep your roots**
> **Grow green your leaves**
> **Reclaim for me this home**

Water the plants and add a fertilizer stick or two if you like. Caress their leaves and talk to them for a moment. Then ask for their protection by saying:

> **By Fire of sun, by drops of Rain**
> **By breath of Air, and Earthly plane**
> **Rosemary plants, now weave your spell**
> **Guard me and mine, and this home well**

Remember to tend the plants personally on a regular basis, and they will tend to you.

## Proving Your Claim

After performing the Rosemary Ritual, walk to the front door, close your eyes, and go in. Then open your eyes and take note of the first thing you see. Is it something of yours? Is it warm and welcoming? If the answer to either of these questions is no, then it's time to make some changes.

Before you can truly reclaim the home, the universe needs to understand that you mean business. That's why it's important that the first thing someone sees when entering the house is an item that belongs to you. It underscores your intention and sets things in motion. It's also a subtle way of telling family members and visitors that a new day has dawned and, while you're happy to share your home with them, you are now in charge.

So, what sort of item should you use? The form it takes isn't important, so it can be anything you like. A picture, a wall hanging, a vase, or a grouping of interesting objects are all good choices. There are only two requirements. It should be an expression of your tastes, your sentiments, and your personality, and of course, it should make others feel welcome.

Making this minor change in decor not only returns the home to you, but works wonders for the personal mindset. It has a way of bringing control to seemingly unmanageable home situations, focus to apathetic family members, and a general harmony into the family unit. And best of all, it brings peace of mind to the mistress of the house. And that's something we could all use a hefty dose of in this busy world.

## Dealing with the Spirit of the House

Sometimes, reclaiming the home takes more than a rosemary plant and a few changes in decor. You may have to make friends with the home spirit. Yes, houses have spirits just like we do. Unlike the human spirit, though, home spirits are born of a culmination of the energies of all the individuals who have lived within the structure. These energies fuse and meld together until they form a living entity that resides within the home. It guards and protects the occupants and, to a large degree, creates the atmosphere others feel when they enter your sanctuary.

Home spirits have individual personalities, unique energies, and firm likes and dislikes. Some are passive, moving about in silent secrecy. Others like to make themselves known, running through the house with so much vim and vigor they could be mistaken for the pesky poltergeist. In any case, all home spirits are possessive of their occupants.

Occasionally, problems with the home spirit will arise when one family moves out and a new one moves in. Why? Because the spirit is used to the lifestyle of the previous family. It's probably spent its whole life tending to them, their wants and needs, and sharing in their joys and sorrows.

When its family leaves, the home spirit becomes confused, befuddled, and hurt. It doesn't have a clue as to the needs of the new occupants, and really isn't sure that it wants to. All it knows is that the family it loved is gone, and that a set of strangers is invading its precious realm. Depending on the personality of the spirit, this can result in sleepless nights, uncomfortable feelings, and missing items for the new occupants.

When I moved into my present home, the spirit was very unhappy. The house had been occupied by the same family for twenty years, and then by twin sisters of that brood for the next fifty. Obviously, the home spirit was very attached to that family, and sadly, my lifestyle was nothing like theirs. In desperation, the spirit tried to whip me into shape.

I suddenly found myself cleaning, wiping, and polishing, not just from time to time but every waking moment. Guests sharing coffee around my kitchen table suddenly took on a gossipy, self-righteous attitude and began behaving as if they were having high tea at the social club. My chain-smoking friends, worried that they might dirty an ash-tray, didn't smoke as much, and their kids took on a "be-seen-and-not-heard" attitude. I began falling asleep at eight o'clock each night and ris-ing every morning at four. After a month or two, I was so exhausted I could barely hold my head up.

Realizing this couldn't go on any longer, I tried reasoning with the home spirit. I explained that I could not live its lifestyle and offered a compromise. But I was dealing with the stubborn sort. My words fell on deaf spirit ears. I tried demanding that it behave so I could live my life. That didn't work either. Finally I took desperate measures—mea-sures that I share with you only to illustrate how a little creativity can bring prompt cooperation, even from the spirit world.

I consecrated the house by asperging its every corner with a mix-ture of bourbon and water and a light sprinkling of cigarette ashes. Then I called in the neighborhood kids and let them run screaming and yelling through the house.

The changes in atmosphere were immediate, and my life resumed its normal flow. Friends no long bitched about each other over coffee, kids were kids again, and (thank the Crone!) my urge to clean every-thing in sight subsided. Even the fatigue vanished. That unorthodox consecration ritual was the most successful magic I've ever performed.

## The Home Spirit Candle

Even though the ritual brought my life back into the norm, it didn't help the home spirit much. Still upset as ever, it just crumpled up in a corner, not knowing what to do. It wasn't familiar with me or my tac-tics. It no longer felt that it belonged, and its feelings were hurt.

As a result, I faced a whole new problem. A profound feeling of sadness pervaded my home. I couldn't allow that to go on either. Somehow, I had to make the spirit feel comfortable and give it a new sense of belonging. The solution? I honored the spirit with a home spirit candle ceremony.

A home spirit candle is one that burns continually, meaning that a fresh candle is lit before the old one burns out. For safety reasons, I usually move this candle into my sink or tub if it's going to be left burning unsupervised. I encourage you to do the same. And for economical reasons, I like to use seven-day candles. These tall candles, which come in glass containers, are easily obtainable at occult shops, flea markets, and sometimes even at grocery stores. White is a good color choice, for all home spirits benefit from its symbolic purity and multifaceted essence.

The only rule for the candle ceremony is that it should reflect your lifestyle. This lets the home spirit know that, regardless of past circumstances, it is now an integral part of your present environment. The idea is to get the spirit to adjust to the new situation while making it feel welcome. If you're a spur-of-the-moment person, you might want to perform a quick, impromptu sort of ritual. This could involve holding the candle in the air and saying something like:

> **Home spirit, I call you and welcome you here**
> **Come join the fun, you've no need to fear**
> **This party's for you; please come be my guest**
> **I offer you love and well wishes and rest**
> **Please continue to protect these surroundings and me**
> **And be a part of my life and my home—Blessed be!**

Place the candle in a prominent spot and light it. Then say a few informal words of welcome to the home spirit. Regardless of what kind of ceremony you perform, one thing is guaranteed. The home spirit will snap out of its blue funk and become your friend.

An added side-effect to this ongoing candle ritual is that it brings an emotionally healthy atmosphere to your living space. Emotional health breeds happiness, security, and a well-adjusted attitude. For that reason alone, I urge you to try this ritual. It's the best way I know to protect yourself, your health, and your home.

# Creating a Personal Sanctuary

All of us need a place to call our own. Because we fill so many roles in the course of a day, this is especially true of women. It doesn't have to be large. It doesn't have to be fancy. It doesn't even have to be a whole room. It only matters that the place is a personal sanctuary, and that no one feels at liberty to encroach on the private moments spent there.

Short of space? A friend with the same problem found her answer beneath the attic staircase. She located a comfortable chair, threw down a few pillows, and added some plants. Then she set up a mini-altar on the window sill. In no time at all, she achieved what she'd dreamed about for years: the luxury of her own sacred space. It was a personal area where she could think, relax, meditate, and kick back. And it was private enough to prevent household intrusion. With a little thought and minimal effort, you can have it, too. Here's what you should consider in order to get started:

- **Location.** Think about where you'd like most to be in your home. This is important because you want your personal place to be enjoyable. Try to find a spot with a window or a skylight. While natural light soothes the spirit, it also goes one step further. It gently nudges the creative juices back into flow without upsetting the state of relaxation you're trying to achieve for body and mind. Don't worry if you can't claim the whole room. Just section off a small portion. In this case, folding screens are wonder workers. They're not only serviceable, they're attractive.

- **Furniture.** Once you've found a spot, consider your tastes in comfort. An overstuffed chair, a bench, or maybe even a hammock might be in order. If you'd rather sit on the floor, consider pillows or a futon. Like the feel of bare floors better? No problem. This is your space, and your comfort is all that matters.

- **Decorating.** Now comes the fun stuff. Gather an assortment of your favorite things and play with decorating ideas. Got a window sill? Try lining it with African violets or stones, or turn it into a mini-altar. Bare corners make ideal spots for hanging plants or drying protective herbs. If space allows, toss in a bookshelf or two. Hang pictures. Nest. Make yourself at home. This is the one area in the home where no one else's decorating tastes come into play, so have fun and allow it to become a total reflection of you.

- **Sense-therapy.** Music and aromatherapy are to the ears and nose what interior design is to the eyes. Now is no time to leave them out. Locate an old tape player or cd changer, and fill a basket with your favorite tunes. Bring in an assortment of incense, scented candles, or essential oils. These items not only soothe overworked senses but go a long way toward creating the total state of relaxation you're trying to achieve.

## ❖ Personal Space Blessing

When your sanctuary is ready, take a little time to dedicate and bless it. Put on some tunes, light a candle and some incense, and stand in the center of the area. Stretch your arms to the ceiling and say something like:

**This is my shelter, this is my space**
**Go away, outside world; in here, you've no place**
**No problems, no worries, no small aggravations**
**Can enter this place of sheer relaxation**
**This is my place, it's my space alone**
**I claim it for Spirit Self, myself, and Crone**

Complete the ritual by spending some time kicking back and relaxing in your new-found sanctuary.

## ❖ Nurturing the New You Ritual

It's time for a pat on the back. By the time you read this, you've accomplished things that take most folks an entire lifetime. You've improved your self-image, waged war on the Analyst, balanced your personality, and taken back your life. Even better, you've single-handedly tossed every bandit who so much as dared to touch your energy supply right out on its rumpus. Great job! You deserve a treat.

Give yourself a present. The gift you choose is important because it's an award to commemorate a momentous occasion—a sort of graduation ceremony. Don't worry if you can't afford an expensive gift. Monetary value is of no consequence here; all that matters is that the item makes you feel special. Best of all, it can take any form you like as long as it's something you can keep with you on a regular basis. A symbolic piece of jewelry, a key ring, or a small pouch of stones or herbs might fit the bill.

Make a list of all your favorite foods, and plan a special evening meal for yourself. After all, no awards ceremony is complete without a banquet. Just this once, don't concern yourself with balancing the four food groups—unless, of course, balanced meals make you jump for joy. The idea is to treat yourself to something scrumptious and luscious, something that makes your mouth water. No matter what trips your trigger, including junk food, Chinese take-out, pizza, or whatever, go for it. And while you're working up the menu, don't forget to add something sweet. You'll need it for the ceremony.

Next, take a long, luxurious bath. Visualize the soap and water rinsing away your old cocoon and any remnants of dysfunctionalism from your life. Feel the power of new life emerging as you relive the rebirthing process. Apply your favorite scent and dress in something that makes you feel good about yourself. Before you sit down to eat, open your arms wide and say:

**Welcome Elements, Crone, and all deities**
**To this rite of emergence and pure gaiety**
**I am fresh, I am new, I'm empowered and strong**
**Come, join in the party and celebrate long**

Lay your hands over the food and drink, and visualize strength, good health, foresight, and happiness flowing into every molecule. Eat slowly and savor each bite. Know that every forkful and every sip empowers the new you to grow in strength and form.

After you've consumed the main course, hold the sweet food item in your hand and think about all the wondrous things life has to offer. Close your eyes and visualize all of life's joys and pleasures flowing into that food. Then open your eyes and say:

**All the sweetness in life is mine now to taste**
**I accept it with pleasure and fully embrace**
**The good I deserve and the joys and fun times**
**I have worked hard to earn them, and now they are mine**

As you eat the item, open yourself up to the joys, happiness, and new opportunities that you deserve. Know that  they await you and are yours for the taking. Then, hold your awards gift in both hands and say:

**I give this to myself; a noble award**
**For outstanding achievement and victory in war**
**With this token of strength, I'm empowered and free**
**My life is my own; I belong just to me**

Feel the power of the gift. Touch it to your third eye, your lips, and your heart. If it's something you can wear, put it on. If not, take symbolic action to make the award your own. For example, you might put keys on a key ring, write your name in a notebook, or put a pouch in your pocket. You get the idea.

Thank the Crone, Elements, and deities for attending your award ritual, then go to bed. Before you doze off, say:

**I am new, I am strong, I am fresh, I am free**
**Bring the bountiful goodness that's waiting for me**

Get a good night's sleep. You'll need plenty of rest to handle all the wonders of your new life.

# You are Important

One final note before we close this chapter. You are the most important person in every room you enter. This does not mean that other people are insignificant, or give you license to be arrogant.

Being the most important person in every room means that you take control of your life by refusing to let it control you. It also means that you accept responsibility for your own actions. Most importantly, though, it means that you realize the significance of your own individual strand within the cosmic web. Without it, the cosmic web would cease to exist as we know it and take on some other form. The world would be a different place. The lives of those you know would change irrevocably, and not necessarily for the best.

Much depends upon the most important person in every room. It is a difficult role filled with the challenges and adventures of the unknown. It isn't always fun but, like everything else worthwhile in this life, its rewards are always sweet. So go ahead. Give it a whirl. Be the most important person in every room. Seize the day, take what life has to offer, and assume your new role. After all, you deserve it.

# Chapter 6

# Healing the Self: Becoming the Crone

If you're reading this chapter, you already know that menopause is a party and not some dread disease. You know that it's as natural a part of the feminine celebratory cycle as birth, puberty, pregnancy, and motherhood. So, why even discuss healing? Because although it has its rewards, menopause (just like the other transitions) also has its rough spots. These rough spots often manifest in physical and emotional symptoms and, when they do, they can be a real bitch.

## You've Got to Be Kidding

We've all heard it millions of times. It's that silly little cliché Mom always used when we thought the sky was falling. The idiotic little phrase that someone uttered when everything was going to hell in a handbasket. The statement that made us want to slap the face right off of whoever had the nerve to say it. Give up? I'll spell it out.

*"Laughter is the best medicine."*

Though this cliché usually invades our lives at what we think are the most inopportune times, no truer statement was ever written. Laughter *is* the best medicine, even for menopause. The ultimate key to a smooth transition is maintaining a good sense of humor. But how can we do that? Some of the symptoms aren't just irritating, they're downright scary. True enough, but no matter how frightening something is, there's always a lighter side. All we have to do is look for it.

Take hot flashes, for instance. One of my girlfriends tells a story about being roped into a blind date. She didn't want to go, but finally resolved herself to the fact there was no way out. Just as the doorbell rang, a hot flash took over. When she opened the door, she was sweating like a pig. Her date, thinking she was coming down with an awful strain of the flu, made a hasty retreat. She was spared what might have been the most boring night of her life. And all it took was one little misunderstood hot flash.

There's humor to be found in other symptoms, too. For example, what do you call a menopausal woman with vaginal yeast overgrowth? An old "sour puss." Yes, it hits close to home. But it's still funny. Once we learn to joke about our symptoms, laugh about them, and see the amusement there, they become less important. And once they become less important, their power over us dissipates. Before we know it, they simply don't bother us any more.

Granted, there may be times when the funny side of this transition escapes you. In that case, talk to other women experiencing the transition or find a menopausal support group. Their stories will give you pause for thought and leave you rolling on the floor. But be careful not to laugh too hard. You just might wet your pants!

# Diet

The word "diet" and I go back a long way and we've never been friends. Every time I saw the word in conjunction with menopause, I just groaned and turned the page. I never even bothered to take a look at the recommendations because I knew what they'd say. "Eat less." "Never put more in your stomach than you can hold in two hands." "Starve and be healthy."

Now, to a girl growing up in a German/Bohemian community, those are fighting words. I knew there were thousands of large women successfully managing menopause everyday, and none of them were going hungry. I didn't intend to, either. To me, eating was more than just filling space in an empty stomach. It was a social event. A pleasure. Sometimes, it even evoked an ecstasy all its own. Of course, I thought menopausal diet plans were devised by some wisp of a woman who wanted to take away all my fun.

One day, though, my curiosity got the best of me. I took a real look at some of the related dietary recommendations, and what I found amazed me. Chocolate, the one thing I never dreamed would be listed, was the recommended cure for cravings and bingeing. Red meat was okay to eat, too. In fact, all my favorite foods were listed. Best of all, though, there were very few no-no's. I could eat whatever I wanted whenever I wanted. I just had to add a few things to my diet each day, and most of them were foods I already enjoyed.

Eventually, I tried a few of the tips. I used what worked for me and discarded the rest. Then I worked up a plan that I could live with. As a result, the hot flashes and night sweats became manageable, my energy levels increased, and nervous tension became a thing of the past. If these symptoms are a problem for you, please try the tips below. You'll feel better than you have in years, and you won't ever be hungry. I promise!

## The No-no's

- **Alcohol.** If you don't drink alcohol now, don't start. If you do, drink in moderation. The liver is the body's main filtering source, and it uses nutrients and minerals to prevent toxins from circulating through your system. To a large degree, it's the organ that holds disease at bay and keeps you from getting sick. Alcohol is difficult for the liver to detoxify. Drinking just one glass of hard alcohol causes the liver to disperse nearly twenty percent of your essential nutrients and prevents them from being used where they're needed most.

- **Caffeine.** Avoid drinking coffee or other caffeinated beverages. Caffeine robs the body of iron. What's more, there's a natural oil in coffee beans that tends to stimulate hot flashes. I have to admit I had trouble with this one. I drink lots of coffee, and doing without it makes me really grumpy. Most of my friends feel the same way about their soft drinks. If you can't do without your daily dose of caffeine, take an iron supplement. To relieve the hot flashes caused from your coffee, drink one cup of All-purpose Tea and take one tablespoon of Good-for-you Vinegar (recipes, page 178) every day.

- **Smoking.** No matter where we look, someone is always reminding us of cigarette-related dangers. One of the main reasons we worry about it in connection with menopause is because nicotine absorbs the body's vitamin C supply and prevents it from being dispersed into the tissues that need it most. As bad as that is, though, menopause doesn't present a good time for heavy smokers to quit. The reasoning behind this is that you have enough physical changes going on without adding the aggravation of symptomatic withdrawal. If you smoke, cut back a bit and take vitamin C. A little vitamin C never hurt anyone, and taken daily, it can also prevent colds.

## Pumping Up the Iron

One of the most common side effects of menopause is loss of iron. This deficiency makes us tired, cranky, and listless. It can also cause memory loss and slow the thinking process. The quickest way to solve the iron deficiency problem and revitalize the mind and body is to eat red meat every day.

Although you can get a good daily supply of iron from plants and their byproducts, they just don't do the job as well as the iron contained in red meats. Here's why. Our bodies consist of red meat, and the iron we naturally manufacture closely resembles the iron structure of other "red meat" animals. Because of this, we are able to absorb the iron from red meat (heme-iron) very quickly. Plant iron, on the other hand, is structured differently. This means that it doesn't work well by itself, and needs help to stay in the body long enough for proper absorption. It latches on to any heme-iron present in the body and stays there until it can be used. When there's no heme-iron available for a piggy-back ride, most of the plant irons are simply flushed away with other waste fluids.

While we need the benefits of red meat during menopause, most of us worry about the cholesterol and fat content. After all, we're constantly told that it's bad for us. True enough, beef is high in both cholesterol and fat. However, wild game is not. If you have a hunter in your family, take advantage of the seasonal harvest. Venison, elk, caribou, rabbit, and squirrel are all high in iron, and won't leave your fat and cholesterol levels sky-rocketing.

I realize this is a tough one for vegans and vegetarians. Even if you take a daily iron supplement to solve the problem, most of the good ones contain animal products. The best bet is to eat plants high in iron, like dandelion greens or blackberries, before your body slows its natural iron-making process. In lieu of that, try a daily dose of B-complex vitamins. Though they won't help as much as red meat, these vitamins do allow some piggy-backing and will keep the plant iron in your system longer.

## Waging War on Osteoporosis

Another common menopausal problem is loss of calcium. Milk consumption alone won't solve this problem because during menopause, the bones begin to lose some of their absorption ability. This means that most of the calcium derived from milk can't be put to use. Instead, it winds up in the soft tissues and just sits there until it turns to fat. This results in loss of bone mass—a problem commonly known as *osteoporosis.*

Osteoporosis is serious business. When bones aren't strong enough to stand erect, they can shift and twist. This causes the body to lose its natural height, and can eventually result in all sorts of problems, including curvature of the spine, hunchback disorder, and arthritis, just to name a few. Most women lose at least ten percent of their bone mass during the first four or five years of menopause. Knowing that the menopausal transition can last for twenty years or more doesn't make for a very pretty picture. Fortunately, there are some things we can do to prevent osteoporosis before it occurs, and keep it in check if it already has.

## Tips to Avoid Osteoporosis

- Eat at least one serving of oatmeal every day. It's high in calcium and bones absorb it more readily than dairy products. If you don't like plain oatmeal, dress it up a bit. Try a little butter, some brown sugar, walnuts, and raisins.

- Bask in the sun. Sunshine is very high in vitamin D, the vitamin necessary for optimum calcium absorption. Ten minutes of sunshine a day gives you the recommended daily requirement.

- Refuse to fall victim to stress. Stress doesn't just cause anxiety; it releases hormones that can actually break down bone mass. To prevent this, try your favorite stress-relieving exercises or refer to the aromatherapy section below.

- Eat two apples every day. Apples contain a mineral called boron that not only helps to ward off osteoporosis but decreases its effects even in the disease's advanced stages. The boron contained in two apples is enough to do the trick.

- Add yogurt to your diet. It's rich in calcium and easily absorbed, so it's great for your bones. It also helps combat vaginal dryness. Don't like plain yogurt? No sweat. Buy any flavor that appeals to you, and add fruit if you like. For something different, add a few blackberries. They're packed with iron—so much so that many herbalists recommend them to anemia patients.

- Take a calcium tablet every day. Menopausal women need 1500 milligrams each day to replace the calcium they lose during this transition. If possible, find a tablet that contains oyster or egg shell in its ingredient list. These types of calcium are more easily absorbed into the bones.

- Exercise. Because it strengthens bones, most physicians recommend some form of daily weight-bearing exercise for women with osteoporosis. The options are endless. Aerobics, dancing, and weight-lifting all fit into this category. If you don't like to exercise, though, don't worry. You can get all the weight-bearing exercise you need during your daily wisdom walk.

- Strengthen your Earth Element (see Chapter 1).

- Ask yourself the following questions. Take steps to rectify any problems you see.

  1. What is lacking in my personal foundations system? Home sector? Work sector? Love sector? Spirituality sector?

  2. Am I too set in my ways? What can I do to become more flexible?

# The Sixty-four
# Thousand Dollar Question

Is hormone replacement therapy (HRT) a miracle cure-all? Or is it the purest form of poison on the prescription market? Opinions vary, not just from doctor to doctor, but from one woman to the next. One thing's for sure, though. HRT is the most talked-about menopausal topic in existence. While HRT seems to successfully handle all sorts of menopausal complaints (hot flashes, night sweats, lack of sexual desire, and so on) it's a therapy that's unproven and may cause more harm than good. Here's why. The liver's job is to filter out any matter foreign to the body. Because HRT is a synthetic substance, the liver's first reaction is to get rid of it. When the liver can't eliminate the HRT, it has no choice but to process it. This action causes a good deal of stress and strain on the liver, and can eventually cause irreparable damage.

The worst problem, though, is the contradictory advice found in published medical reports. Some medical researchers say that HRT can actually cause heart disease, kidney disorders, breast cancer, and a variety of other horrors. Other researchers contend that the findings of their colleagues are nothing more than nonsensical ramblings coupled with psycho-babble. Of course, that doesn't help us any. When the experts can't even agree on whether synthetic HRT is safe or not, there's no way in the world we can make any sort of sound decision about using it.

Fortunately, there are other options. A natural form of estrogen, commonly known as phytoestrogen, is also found in a good many plants. Though its effects aren't as strong and don't work as quickly as synthetic HRT, it bonds easily to the body's hormone receptors and targets the tissues that need its benefits. This means it doesn't confuse the liver, overwork it, or damage it in any way. Even better, there are no reports of disease-causing side effects. I think it's a much safer solution all the way around.

If you choose to try phytoestrogen therapy, just remember that a daily pill or monthly shot won't do the trick. You'll have to introduce certain plants into your meals, your snacks, and your beverages. Also, you will not see immediate results. It often takes a month or so of diligent, uninterrupted therapy before any changes become apparent. Don't get discouraged or allow frustration to take over. Just know that phytoestrogen therapy does work, and that millions of women use it successfully every day.

Many health food stores carry phytoestrogen in pill form. The only drawback to this type of therapy is the number of supplements you'll have to swallow. Often the recommended dosage is six to eight pills (sometimes more) three times a day. And after you've consumed that many pills, you may not feel like eating anything else at all.

An easier solution is to incorporate phytoestrogens into your daily meal plans. There are literally thousands of common plants that contain phytoestrogen, and finding and preparing them isn't as much trouble as you might think. For example, soy beans are very rich in phytoestrogen, and every supermarket on the planet carries them. Best of all, they come in a variety of forms, products, and derivatives: tofu, crackers, and meat substitutes, just to name a few. Other plants high in phytoestrogen include alfalfa sprouts, red clover blossoms, and flax seeds. These are easily obtainable, too, and make tasty additions to soups, salads, and sandwiches. To boost phytoestrogen throughout the day, drink a between-meals tea of dong quai,[6] black cohosh,[7] and licorice.[8] It's delicious, it increases your metabolism, and it provides the energy necessary for today's busy lifestyle.

# Simple Remedies for Menopausal Miscellany

The following is a list of common menopausal complaints and some simple things you can do at home to relieve them. Be sure to work with the sets of questions related to your symptoms. Your responses may uncover blocked areas of your life that feed your symptoms' energy, keeping them active. Incorporate the healing chants, too. Even

6, 7, 8. See footnotes, page 229.

though they may seem silly at first, they are very powerful. Used daily, they can bring great success.

If symptoms persist or worsen, don't hesitate to seek the advice of your homeopath or family doctor. After all, healing is their business, too. There's always a chance that something other than normal menopausal changes are complicating your transitional symptoms.

## Aching Joints

- For quick relief, try a ginger bath. Infuse one ounce of powdered ginger in six cups of water, using the general infusion instructions on page 179. Add the infusion to a hot bath and soak until the water starts to cool.

- Take a teaspoonful of evening primrose oil three times a day.

- Take twenty drops of ginseng, sarsaparilla, or black cohosh tincture daily. For general herbal tincture instructions, see page 180.

- Carry a charged opal. Enchant it by saying something like:

**Ever-changing fluid stone**
**Ease the aches inside my joints and bones**

- Strengthen your Water Element (see Chapter 1).

- Ask yourself the following questions. Take steps to rectify any problems you see.

    1. Do I accept new ideas and perceptions freely, or am I locked into my own personal mindset?

    2. Have I thoroughly embraced and welcomed the freedoms of the menopausal transition?

    3. Am I willing to admit my mistakes and rectify them?

- Daily chant:

**Aches in joints, go now! Retreat!**
**Come now, ease of movement sweet**
**Fluid motion return to me**
**As I will, so mote it be**

## Bingeing

- Eat a chocolate bar. It may surprise you to know that chocolate is filled with a hefty supply of minerals. That's what you're lacking when you have the urge to binge.

- Listen to your body. If you crave something, no matter how weird it may seem, eat it. Tending to cravings right away prevents bingeing later.

- Add chromium to your diet. Good sources include beets, liver, mushrooms, nuts, and whole wheat.

- Drink yarrow tea. Infuse one teaspoon dried yarrow in one cup of water. Sweeten with molasses.

- Carry a charged blue topaz. Enchant it by saying something like:

**Stone that quenches appetite**
**Stay my urge to binge with all your might**

- Strengthen your Air Element (see Chapter 1).

- Answer the following questions. Take steps to rectify any problems you see.

    1. What blessings have I refused to let into my life?

   2. Why do I sacrifice my needs for the needs of others?

   3. Why do I willingly take on more than I can handle, rather than expect others to do their fair share?

- Daily chant:

**Binges, you're not good for me**
**So go away and let me be**
**I eat what I want in moderation**
**Leaving no room for exacerbation**

## High Blood Pressure

- Reduce your salt intake. If food tastes bland without extra salt, try seasoning with a little lemon juice or black pepper instead.

- Add potassium to your diet. Excellent sources include bananas, broccoli, cabbage, carrots, orange juice, and wheat. In addition to relieving high blood pressure, potassium prevents and relieves muscle cramps.

- Infuse one teaspoon of dried feverfew in one cup of water. Sweeten with molasses and drink daily.

- Eat raw garlic. For a twist, add it to baked potatoes, scrambled eggs, pasta, and tomato juice.

- Ground and center. Sit comfortably and inhale positive energy from the Earth; then exhale fully, dispelling all negative energy from your body. Focus on your breathing until every fiber of your being relaxes.

- Carry a charged amethyst with you. Enchant it by saying something like:

**Stone that makes short work of stress**
**Bring me peace and calm and happiness**

- Strengthen your Earth Element (see Chapter 1).

- Ask yourself the following questions. Take steps to rectify any problems you see.

  1. What steps am I taking to manage my personal stress?

  2. What can I do to slow down and stop rushing through life?

  3. Do I try to force others to share my personal views?

- Daily chant:

**Calm, rich energy of Mother Earth**
**Bring back laughter, smiles, and mirth**
**Liken the pressure in my veins**
**To the steady flow of gentle rains**

## Fatigue

- Drink at least one cup of ginseng tea each day. Use one teaspoon of dried ginseng to each cup of water.

- Take bee pollen daily, and add riboflavin (B-2) to your diet. Good sources of riboflavin are alfalfa sprouts, beans, dairy products, dandelion greens, mushrooms, onions, parsley, and peppermint.

- Exercise daily. Though it sounds like a contradiction in terms, exercise and fatigue really do mix. If you like, add five or ten minutes to your daily wisdom walking. You'll be surprised at the extra energy you'll have.

- Carry a charged quartz crystal with you. Enchant it by saying:

**Stone of energy and perfect power**
**Increase my endurance by minute and hour**

- Strengthen your Fire Element (see Chapter 1).

- Ask yourself the following questions. Take steps to rectify any problems you see.

  1. What in my life is cause for depression? Anxiety? Stress?

  2. Which areas of my life need growth and nurturing? What can I do to help them blossom?

  3. Why do I willingly accept the negative energy of other people into my life?

- Daily chant:

**Physical energy, come to me**
**Bring vigor, endurance, and vitality**
**Increase my stamina three times three**
**As I will, so mote it be**

## Incontinence

- Don't hold it. If you have to urinate, find a bathroom right away. Putting it off only compounds the problem. It weakens the bladder walls and causes tiny blisters. When the blisters break, and they will, wetting your pants will be the least of your problems. Urine will seep out into your body, poisoning your whole system.

- Use the double-void system. Empty your bladder completely. Then apply pressure to the pelvic area to release leftover fluids.

- Drink large quantities of cranberry juice or chamomile tea. These not only curb the problem, but also ward off bladder infections.

- Take fifteen drops of black cohosh tincture twice a day as needed.

- Carry a charged hematite with you. Enchant it by saying:

**Stone of iron, so silvery sleek**
**Hold body wastes tightly so they don't leak**

- Strengthen your Air and Earth Elements (see Chapter 1).

- Ask yourself the following questions. Take steps to rectify any problems you see.

  1. Am I living my own life, or am I allowing someone else's views to leak over on me and color my personal path?

  2. Do I stand up for myself, my rights, and my personal beliefs?

  3. What can I do to become less wishy-washy?

- Daily chant:

**Bladder, hold what's meant to be**
**Work to your capacity**
**Let no leaks or seepage creep**
**Until I find a toilet seat**

## Memory Loss

- Don't take on more than you can handle. Feeling overwhelmed only makes the problem worse.

- Make a "to do" list. Add to the list as you think of things that need your attention, and cross off tasks as you finish them.

- Infuse one teaspoon of dried ginkgo in one cup of water. Drink two cups of infusion daily. Sweeten with molasses.

- Take thirty drops of sage tincture twice a week.

- Carry a charged fluorite. Enchant it by saying something like:

> **Precious stone of knowledge gained**
> **Keep my memory clear and plain**

- Strengthen your Air and Fire Elements (see Chapter 1).

- Ask yourself the following questions. Take steps to rectify any problems you see.

  1. Which areas of my life seem to be stuck in a rut?

  2. What can I do to more freely express myself and communicate my feelings more effectively?

  3. Do I have any mental blocks? What can I do to remove them?

- Daily chant:

> **Brain, work with me on this day**
> **Bring memory back and let it stay**
> **Save all knowledge that I've gained**
> **And what I learn now, please retain**

## Uterine Cramps, Excessive Bleeding

- Drink feverfew or rosemary tea as needed. Infuse one teaspoon of dried herb in one cup of water. Sweeten with molasses.

- Eat peppermint candy. If you're a diabetic, try a cup of peppermint tea instead. Infuse as directed for the teas above.

- Take vitamin A. Good sources are milk and animal liver. There are unfortunately no plant sources for this vitamin.

- Carry a charged moonstone with you. Enchant it by saying something like:

**Stone of women, moon, and tides**
**Let this discomfort now subside**

- Strengthen your Earth and Air Elements (see Chapter 1).

- Ask yourself the following questions. Take steps to rectify any problems you see.

    1. How am I giving away my personal power?

    2. What can I do to break the bonds I've imposed on myself?

    3. Why do I punish myself when I make a mistake?

- Daily chant:

**Uterus, come be my friend**
**And let this angry cramping end**
**Hear my words and please allow**
**This bloody flood to stop right now**

## Weight Gain

- Add psyllium seed and alfalfa sprouts to your diet. Because they swell in the stomach, they give a feeling of fullness and keep you from being hungry between meals.

- If water retention is a problem, add one tablespoon of cider vinegar to a full glass of water. Drink two glasses a day.

- Once a week, for two consecutive days, eat nothing but broiled steak and fresh tomatoes. These add bulk and fiber, and help to flush the system.

- Use honey or molasses in place of sugar.

- Carry a charged blue topaz with you. Enchant it by saying something like:

> **Bluest stone of strength and diet**
> **Still hunger pangs—make them be quiet**

- Strengthen your Fire Element (see Chapter 1).

- Ask yourself the following questions. Take steps to rectify any problems you see.

  1. Which areas of my life have I put on hold? What can I do to revitalize them?

  2. How can I reactivate my talents and make good use of them?

  3. What am I holding on to that I should release from my life?

- Daily chant:

> **Crone blood is wise—I hold it in**
> **It neither makes me fat nor makes me thin**
> **All negative energy I now dispel**
> **With it, weight gain flees as well**

## Yeast Infection

- Use a douche of one cup plain yogurt to one quart warm water.

- Avoid bubble baths and scented soaps until the infection dissipates. These can complicate the problem. Instead, add ½ quart of apple cider vinegar to your bath, or take a sitz bath. This brings vaginal acids back into balance and provides instant itch relief.

- Since tight-fitting garments tend to aggravate yeast infections, you should refrain from wearing panties. If you must wear them, only wear those with absorbent cotton crotches.

- Infuse one ounce dried red clover blossoms in six cups of water. Drink three cups daily to treat infection. Sweeten with molasses.

- Carry a charged blue lace agate with you. Enchant it by saying something like:

**Stone of feminine power and healing**
**Balance my fluids and send yeast reeling**

- Strengthen your Water Element (see Chapter 1).

- Ask yourself the following questions. Take steps to rectify any problems you see.

    1. Have I allowed my spirituality to stagnate, or do I embrace its ever-changing role in my life?

    2. What am I doing to heal the hurts, wounds, and scars of my past?

    3. What can I do to manage my life better and bring balance back into the areas I've let slide?

- Daily chant:

**Vaginal yeast, you cannot stay**
**Your growth and itch must cease today**
**I steal your power—you must flee**
**As I will, so mote it be**

## ❖ General Good Health Ritual

On rising each morning, take a glass of juice to your personal space. Light a white candle and your choice of incense. Greet your personal Crone with a toast, then ask for Her protection by saying something like:

> **Strongest Crone, You Who protects**
> **The beings of this gentle sex**
> **Smile on me and guard my health**
> **Bring peace of mind and all the wealth**
> **That happiness and wholeness brings**
> **Chase my symptoms and their stings**
> **Far away from me this day**
> **And let me live and work and play**
> **In healthful comfort as You guide**
> **My steps today; stay at my side**
> **And lovingly watch over me**
> **My dearest Crone—Blessed be**

Drink the juice and relax for a few minutes. Then snuff out the candle and start your day.

# Recipes for Infusions and Tinctures

When using herbal remedies, always try to use fresh plant materials or herbs that you've dried yourself. The fact is that most of the herbal capsules found in health food stores are fairly ineffective. This is because they're usually made with powdered herbs, and herbs reduced to powder lose power long before fresh or dried ones. Besides, there's no way to tell how long it sat on the shelf before you bought it. You may be buying little more than a placebo. If you can't grow or dry your own, purchase dried herbs in bulk. They're very inexpensive and easily acquired through any good herbal mail order company. For your convenience, some of my favorites are listed at the end of this section.

# General Note for Making Infusions

All of the herb proportions listed in recipes for infusions in the treatment sections are written with the assumption that you'll be using dried plant materials. When using fresh herbs, you should double the recommended amount. This is because the nutrients contained in dried plant materials are twice as concentrated than those found in fresh plants.

## Coffee Maker Infusions

Put a fresh coffee filter in the filter basket of the coffee maker, and add the recommended amount of plant material. Then brew a full pot of water. Allow the infusion to sit for five to ten minutes after the brew stops dripping, then use. Don't throw away any left over infusion. It keeps well in the refrigerator for up to two weeks. If you like it warm, you can always nuke it later.

## Standard Infusions

Using a glass pot, bring the recommended amount of water to a rolling boil. Remove heat, add the plant material, and cover. Let sit for at least one hour, then use.

## Herbal Tinctures

To make a tincture, fill a jar with chopped, dried plant material, and pour 100-proof vodka over it. Then cap, label, and let steep for six weeks. Use five ounces of vodka for every one ounce of plant material. Mix the recommended dosage in a cup of warm water and drink.

## All-purpose Tea

1 teaspoon catnip
1 teaspoon chamomile
1 teaspoon passionflower
1 teaspoon lemon balm
$^1/_2$ teaspoon peppermint leaves
4 cups water

Bring herbs and water to a boil and remove from heat. Let steep for fifteen minutes, strain, and drink.

## Good-for-you Vinegar

Dandelion roots and leaves
Plantain leaves
Red clover blossoms *or* nettle leaves
Cider vinegar

Fill a quart jar with the plant materials listed above. Dried will work, but fresh is better. Add cider vinegar until the liquid reaches the jar neck. Place plastic wrap over the jar opening and cap tightly. Label and keep in a dark place for six weeks. This vinegar is terrific when sprinkled liberally on fish or used as a salad dressing. Or, for a warm drink, add a tablespoon to a cup of hot water and flavor it with molasses.

# Herbal Mail Order Resources

Each company listed below provides superior quality herbs at reasonable prices with a quick turn-around. When inquiring by mail, please include a self-addressed stamped envelope.

**Ancient Ways**
4075 Telegraph Road
Oakland, CA 94609
510-653-3244

**The Enchanted Apothecary**
72-01 Austin Street
Forest Hills, NY 11375
1-800-865-5006

**Hourglass Creations**
2377 Kensington Ave.
Amherst, NY 14226

**Mountain Rose Herbs**
P.O. Box 2000
Redway, CA 95560
1-800-879-3337

# Aromatherapy: Good Scents for Attitude

Although sass is a multi-faceted magic that works wonders with any attitude, it can't cure everything all by itself. Sometimes, it needs a boosting agent of sorts—a companion remedy. One of the best boosters in existence is aromatherapy. Aromatherapy is just that: a therapy involving aromas.

As we smell certain scents, the nose sends a message to the brain. It tells the brain that we feel better, the brain tells the rest of the body and, before long, we're back in sync again. It's a quick, effective cure. Best of all, there are no pills to take, no mess to make, and nothing to signal that healing is in progress, unless you want to count the wonderful scents swirling around in the atmosphere. There are lots of ways to incorporate this wonderful healing therapy into your life. All methods work equally well.

## Good Scents Methods

- **Inhalation therapy.** Open a bottle of essential oil. Inhale deeply for a few seconds, then chant:

  **Herbal oil, cure what ails**
  **Bring respite now without fail**

- **Light bulb therapy.** Rub a few drops of essential oil on a light bulb, and turn it on. Leave the light on until the aroma permeates the room.

- **Shampoo therapy.** Add a few drops of essential oil to your regular shampoo or conditioner. Then, you can reap its benefits all day.

- **Bath therapy.** Add some essential oils to liquid soap, or make bath oils or salts. For bath oil, add a few drops to a small amount of unscented vegetable or mineral oil. For bath salts, pour a handful of table salt in a resealable bag, and add two or three drops of oil. Give it a good shake, then add it to your bath.

- **Stovetop therapy.** Add a few drops of essential oil to a pot of water and let it simmer on the stove. Don't leave the pot unattended on the stove, and be sure to add water throughout the day.

- **Laundry therapy.** For long-lasting therapy, add a drop or two of essential oil to your washer's rinse cycle, or toss a scented handkerchief in the dryer.

## Quick Reference Aromatherapy Treatment Chart

While aromatherapy is an effective treatment for many ailments, there isn't enough space in this book to list them all. For this reason, the chart below only lists the aroma used to treat the most common menopausal complaints. For other aromatherapy treatments, see the aromatherapy reading list at the end of this section.

| Ailment | Therapeutic Aroma |
| --- | --- |
| Anxiety* | Cinnamon, cloves, lavender, honeysuckle, strawberry |
| Depression | Bergamot, clary sage, grapefruit, jasmine, lavender, lemon, lemon balm, lemon verbena, neroli, peach, rose geranium, sandalwood, strawberry, ylang ylang |
| Fatigue | Angelica, benzoin, black pepper, camphor, cardamom, cinnamon, basil, clove, cypress, eucalyptus, lemon, peppermint, pine, sage |
| Insomnia | Cinnamon, clove, frankincense, hops, myrrh, neroli, nutmeg, orange, rose, vanilla, violet, ylang-ylang |
| Stress | Bergamot, cedar, cypress, lavender, marjoram, myrrh, orange, peach, rose, violet |

## Aromatherapy Reading List

Cunningham, Scott. *Magical Aromatherapy*. St. Paul, MN: Llewellyn Publications, 1992.

Tisserand, Maggie. *Aromatherapy for Women*. England: Thorson's, Northamptonshire, 1985.

Tisserand, Robert. *The Art of Aromatherapy*. New York: Destiny Books, 1977.

---

* You can be creative with aromatherapy. For instance, to treat anxiety, eat an apple every day—sprinkle each apple slice with cinnamon and cloves, and inhale deeply.

# Acupuncture: An Alternative Treatment

Centuries old, acupuncture is one of the most successful medical treatments available today. Perhaps this is because it works with *ch'i* or the personal life force, which is the combination of yin (the body's female force) and yang (the body's male force). Since ch'i flows through every sector of our beings (physical, mental, emotional, and spiritual), acupuncture treats the whole person—not just the symptom. This is important because underlying, seemingly unrelated problems often block relief from the symptoms that creep to the surface.

The basic premise for acupuncture is a simple one. When the energy flow of the ch'i becomes blocked or unbalanced due to too much yin or too much yang, it signals every sector of our being. We usually don't hear the mental, emotional, or spiritual warnings, so the physical sector notifies us. The first warning signs are subtle, and can manifest in tiredness, minor pain, an occasional sneeze, and so forth. If we ignore these symptoms and don't tend to them immediately, the body has no choice. It doles out a sterner warning by initiating the systematic shutdown of at least one area of the body. In short, we get sick.

Acupuncture works by using fine gauge needles to stimulate certain nerve centers lining the energy paths and feeding areas of ch'i. Upon stimulation, these nerve centers clear the blocked pathways to allow yin and yang to flow properly and put ch'i back in balance. Then they send an electronic impulse to the brain, telling it that we aren't sick anymore. The brain, in turn, shuts down the physical body's warning alarms. Our symptoms go away, and we feel fine again.

The amount of treatment necessary to clear the energy paths and balance the ch'i varies from person to person. A lot depends on your attitude, the amount of happiness you allow into your life, and how much blockage and imbalance you've allowed to accumulate. For example, I've always been able to clear my problems with two or three treatments every few months. My husband, on the other hand, has more difficulty keeping his ch'i in balance. Thus, his treatment plan is much more extensive than mine.

Over the years, I've had great success with acupuncture. I've used it to clear out hip and back pain, menopausal symptoms, and even writer's block. Many people won't try it, though, because they're afraid it might hurt. It doesn't. Fact is, you'll probably never even feel the needles. And if you do, know that the stimulation sensation has less stinging power than the most minor mosquito bite.

Another reason for hesitation is that most folks think that acupuncture is relatively expensive. They're wrong. Price per treatment varies according to living area, but it usually runs between thirty and sixty dollars—about the same as you'd pay for a visit to the family doctor. If you have medical insurance but can't afford the cash outlay, give your insurance company a call. Some of them pay up to seventy percent of all acupuncture charges. You just may be one of the lucky ones.

If this sort of therapy appeals to you, search carefully for a well-established, well-practiced acupuncturist. If you can't find a listing in the yellow pages, don't fret. Many chiropractors are also acupuncturists; they just don't advertise because alternative treatment practitioners haven't reached the same social acceptability enjoyed by those practicing internal and spinal medicines. If you still can't find an acupuncturist in your area, use the acupuncture referral list below.

Once you've found a practitioner, don't be afraid to ask for a list of professional recommendations and patient references. Take the time to phone each one, and ask any questions you might have. If everything checks out, make your first appointment. You'll be glad you did.

## Acupuncture Referral List

If you're having trouble finding a licensed acupuncturist in your area, one of the organizations listed below will be glad to help you. If you've found a practitioner, they can also give you information regarding licensure and credentials.

**American Association of Acupuncture and Oriental Medicine**
433 Front Street
Catasauqua, PA 18032-2506
610-433-2448

**National Alliance of Acupuncture and Oriental Medicine**
638 Prospect Avenue
Hartford, CT 06105
203-586-7509

**National Commission for the Certification of Acupuncturists**
1424 16th Street NW
Suite 105
Washington, DC 20036
202-232-1404

# Acupuncture Reading List

Connelly, Dianne M. *Traditional Acupuncture: The Law of the Five.* Columbia, MD: Center for Traditional Acupuncture, 1979.

Kaptchuk, Ted. *The Web That Has No Weaver.* New York: Congdon and Weed, 1983.

Mitchell, Ellinor R. *Plain Talk About Acupuncture.* New York: Whalehall, Inc., 1987.

# Chapter 7

# Abracadabra: Help with Notions, Commotions, and Devotions

While it's true that you may not need spell props and such for successful magic once you reach menopause, you may want to take advantage of some of the following spell boosters. Not only do they add power to magical efforts, they can assist you in focusing your intent and aid you in directing the flow of energy so it's guaranteed to hit its mark.

## Soaring with Moonbeams, Moonlight, and Dark Skies

The Moon and Her phases provide a perfect environment for every type of spellwork. This is especially true for female practitioners, for we automatically align ourselves to Her silvery, feminine energy. How could we not? From the moment of conception, She captains our personal ships of life. She controls our seas of emotion, the flow of our body fluids, and the tides of our menstrual cycles. She even picks the time we're inducted into Cronehood by insisting that we hold our moon-blood inside and use its potency and power for our own personal gain.

The Moon watches over us and is, in many ways, our friend and mentor. She willingly extends Her energy to boost our magical efforts. All we have to do is ask, and know how to work with Her cycle to get the maximum potency from the energy She lends. The key is to discern which of Her phases best suits the work we wish to perform.

## Moon Phases

- **Waxing Moon.** This is the phase in which the Moon's light grows in the sky from dark to full. This energy works most efficiently when used for growth, enlargement, or general gain. Waxing Moon is the time for efforts involving prosperity, creativity, new endeavors, vitality, and good health. Any issue that requires increase is a good bet.

- **Full Moon.** This is when the Moon's energy is at its peak. Although I like to use this energy for increase as well, it presents a time when virtually any spellwork can meet with success. Save your difficult efforts for this period, or use it for spells that need a super burst of power to reach their target.

- **Waning Moon.** This occurs when the Moon's light diminishes and shrinks from full to dark. Likewise, anything that requires shrinkage, loss, discount, or decrease works well at this time. It's a good time to perform efforts involving weight loss, health problems (especially surgeries), symptom dissipation, breaking bad habits, and so forth.

- **Dark Moon.** This is the time when no Moon appears in the sky. It's a very special time because it belongs solely to the Crone.

Though it's a good time to rest, recoup, and regenerate, it also presents other possibilities. If you prefer to work with magic at this time, use the energy for efforts involving divination, psychism, clairvoyance, meditation, seeing through deception, and uncovering the mysteries.

The magical operations listed above are only suggestions to give you an idea of how specific Moon energies work. They in no way comprise a complete list of available magical options. Use your imagination and explore the possibilities.

# Gathering the Power of Nature

Effective magic relies heavily on intent, focus, and unobstructed energy flow. Gifts of Nature, like plants and stones, can help us in these areas. First, they provide a focal point for magical work. This is important because the mind often needs help to stay on track. Second, they add their energy to the effort, and give it the strength to fly smoothly through the cosmos. Most importantly, though, their energies reinforce our intent and give our efforts shape and definition. This gives the universe a set of specifics to work with; in short, they let the universe know what we want and how we want it to happen. Because Nature's gifts contain both symbolic and intrinsic value, harnessing their energies for magic makes every operation more powerful.

## Herbs: Harnessing the Wild Power

Herbs are the most frequently used plants in the history of the ancient arts. It's probably because they possess an innate strength that most other plants lack. Herbs are little more than common weeds, and they don't need a lot of care to thrive. It doesn't make much difference if you forget to water or feed them. They just go on about the business of living their lives, re-seeding and sprouting wherever they want. In short, herbs are independent, unruly plants with an attitude. When such power is harnessed and incorporated in magic, it brings incredible potency to spellwork.

## Charging Herbs for Magical Use

You can increase the power of herbs by charging them, thereby enhancing whatever magical characteristic they embody that is suitable for your spellwork. Appendix I lists herbs and their magical associations. If you're not familiar with the process of charging herbs, don't worry; just follow these steps:

1. Pour the amount of herb you need for the intended spell into a dish. Place your hands over it until you feel the its energy start to pulsate. Then touch the herb, close your eyes, and focus on the magical intent.

2. Run your fingers through the herb particles. Feel your energy mix with that of the herb. This begins the charging process.

3. To add more power, chant an appropriate line or two as you touch the herb. For instance, if you were charging sage for a general wisdom spell, you might say something like:

Herb of wisdom and mental power<br>Increase my knowledge hour by hour

4. Keep chanting and touching the herbs until the plant material between your fingers begins to tingle. Repeat the process to charge other herbs as necessary.

## Magical Methodologies for Herbs

There are lots of ways to use herbs in magic. Here are a few ideas:

- **Burning.** This is the best way I know to fill the atmosphere with magical intent. Use herbs alone as incense, or add them to an appropriate one. You can also anoint candles in vegetable oil and roll them in herbs that mirror your intent.

- **Carrying.** Herbs are powerful charms. Carry or wear a sprig to amplify your message to the universe. If you like, mix several herbs together and carry them in a sachet.

- **Growing.** Growing herbs at home sends a living, constant message to the cosmos. It serves as a reminder that the related spell is ongoing and infinite.

- **Infusing.** Infusion converts herbs to liquid, which opens a world of opportunity to the practitioner. Add them to your bath, your laundry, or use them as washes to clean the house. You can also drink them as teas. Remember, some herbs are poisonous. Before you ingest any herb, you must check a reliable source to make sure it's safe for human consumption.

- **Powdering.** Powdered herbs used for magic, unlike those used for symptom relief, do not lose their power. Sprinkle them through your house or tie them up in a sachet. For a great body powder, combine them with cornstarch. Be aware that some herbs, like cinnamon, are very strong. If your skin is sensitive, you may want to test a small area before dusting your whole body.

- **Seeding.** For magic requiring transformation, toss charged herb seed on the winds. The transformation begins as soon as the seed begins to sprout.

## Flower Power

Although the energy of flowers is more cultured than that of their herbal siblings, their power is just as potent. This is because flowers evoke strong emotions from humankind, and pure emotion is the center from which all magic flows. We use them to celebrate and commemorate special events like birthdays, weddings, anniversaries, and funerals. Because they symbolize the way we feel, we often send them as tokens of love, appreciation, and honor. No doubt about it, flowers mirror the personal emotional world. Looking at it from this angle, it's little wonder we use them as viable magical tools.

### Magical Methodologies for Flowers

There are many ways to use flower energy in magical efforts. For a list of flowers and their magical associations, see Appendix I. The techniques described for herbs and those listed below work equally well.

- During the Full Moon, carefully wash some magically appropriate flower buds. Remove the stems and float the buds in a full glass of water. The next day, drink the water to receive the magical properties of the flower. As with herbs, some flowers are poisonous. You must check a reliable source (refer to the Bibliography for suggestions) before you use any flowers in this fashion.

- Write a chant, prayer, or incantation on a piece of paper. Place it under the vase of a flower bud appropriate to your magical intent. The spell reaches completion when the bud opens.

- Anoint a seven-day candle and inscribe it with your desire. Place it next to a flower bud in a vase. Let the candle burn until the bud opens. The opening of the bud sets the spell in motion.

## Stones: Stabilizing the Magic

The body of our planet is comprised largely of stones and stone derivatives. Strong and powerful, stones provide us with the foundation we need to live comfortably on the Earth's surface. In short, they bring stability to physical existence. Practitioners often incorporate this powerful, stabilizing energy in their magical efforts for two reasons. First, every stone in existence is ancient. It has seen more than we shall ever see, been places we shall never go, and existed longer than any human body ever can. Stones hold the history of the world within them— every movement, every decision, every smile, and every tear. The antiquity of their nature alone makes them viable magical tools.

Secondly, their power over the human psyche is overwhelming—so much so, in fact, that some people believe stones have the ability choose their owners instead of the other way around. Others believe birthstones bring their wearer good luck, that a commitment of marriage should be sealed with a diamond, and that opals given without love bring chaos and tragedy to their owners.

Stones exude a special type of magic. Much like flowers, they entrance us with their beauty, and easily stir the seas of human emotion. But their magical viability factor goes much deeper. Because they form our foundation, stones provide a link between the physical world and the magical realm. We use them because they stabilize every bit of magic they touch.

## Charging Stones for Magical Use

As with herbs, it's a good idea to charge stones appropriately for the magical task at hand before using them. Refer to Appendix II for a list of stones and their magical associations. An easy method for charging stones is described below.

1. Hold the stone firmly in your dominant hand, then touch it to your third eye.

2. Focus on the magical intent and visualize what you desire to reach fruition.

3. Vocalize your desire. If charging an amethyst for stress relief, for example, you might say something like:

**O purple stone of serenity**
**Relieve all stress that comes to me**

4.  Chant out loud until you feel the stone begin to pulsate. When the charge is complete, the stone will pulse with a steady rhythm.

### Magical Methodologies for Stones

If you feel drawn to stones and want to incorporate them in your magical work, try some of the ideas below.

- Place a stone appropriate to your need in a glass of water, and allow it to steep overnight. The next morning, drink the water to bring its properties into your life. Check a reliable stone reference (see Bibliography) before you do this. Believe it or not, some stones are very toxic.

- During candlemaking, add the appropriate stones while the wax is soft.

- Stones can be powdered and added to incense. To do this, seal the stone in a resealable plastic bag. Put the bag inside several paper sacks, then crush the stone using a hammer.

- Either carry or wear charged stones to get the full benefit of their vibrations.

Collecting a good supply of stones for magical use doesn't have to be expensive. Check your local lapidary for small tumbled pieces. They are just as powerful as expensive faceted stones. Your stone collection doesn't have to be large, either. Many stones contain the same properties, and some, like clear quartz crystal and opal, can be charged for virtually any magical use.

# Communicating with Symbols

Symbols are one of the most powerful spell boosters available to the practitioner. This is because they involve the whole mind instead of just a part of it. First they communicate a message to the unconscious and subconscious portions of the mind. These sectors, in turn, send the message to the conscious mind. Since all the sectors are involved and work together in the thought (messaging) process, a clearer image comes into play. This image can actually change the way we perceive the events in our lives and the way we deal with them.

When we channel focused energy through symbols, the mind automatically forms a list of possibilities and presents it to the higher self. The higher self goes through the list, decides which course of action to take for the desired result, and sets the spell in motion. Then it communicates the action taken to the conscious mind. The conscious mind processes the information and, without even realizing it, we begin to take coordinating steps on a mundane level to bring the magical results we expect.

If you've never incorporated symbols in your magic before, I urge you to give them a shot. It's the easiest way I know to restructure your reality and bring the results that you crave. Use the suggestions in Appendix III to get started, and feel free to add to this list as more symbols come to mind. By doing so, you'll enhance your personal magic and your success rate.

## Engaging the Goddess with Couplets

Contrary to popular belief, the Goddesses we invoke for spellwork during menopause don't have to be Crones. The Mother and Maiden Goddesses are happy to help us as well. We've lived Their phases and successfully completed Their lessons. Thus, we belong to Them and They to us. For this reason, don't hesitate to call on the Goddess of your choice. Reaching Cronehood is no reason to dissolve a solid relationship. But as you go on with your magical life, remember to include a few Crone Goddesses in your work. We can never have too much help or too many friends.

When invoking a deity for magical work, take a little time to write out an invocation or incantation. While informal magic is fine, once in a while deities, especially Goddesses, enjoy a formal invitation more than a half-thrown-together ritual and some flattery. Think about what you want to say, then add a few flourishes.

A good way to accomplish this is to work out your invocations and chants in couplets. Couplets are two lines in which the last words of each line rhyme. They aren't as difficult to work with as you might think. During a wish spell, for example, you might normally say something like:

**Let my wishes fill the atmosphere**
**and fly out into the cosmos**

If you worked the incantation in couplets, though, it might sound something like this:

**Let my wishes fill the sky**
**And out into the cosmos fly**

Though it may take more time to work out your spells in couplet form, the results are well worth the effort. Why? Other than the obvious (the fact that Goddesses like to be coaxed with poetry), there are several reasons.

1. Couplets sound magical. They put you in the proper mood and help you focus on your magical goal.

2. Couplets flow easily; they give magic the impetus necessary for a smooth take-off.

3. Couplets have rhythm—the sort of rhythm that tends to entrance practitioners. They provide the altered state of consciousness necessary for excellent magical results.

Couplets are the glue that binds the spell together. They act as an adhesive bundling agent and connect all parts of a spell securely. This means it reaches its destination fully intact, and that's important for good results.

You don't have to be a poet to write couplets. Anyone can write them. All it takes is a little time. The key to writing them successfully is not to allow the wording to overwhelm you. Remember, even the simplest ditty will do the trick. Just pick up your pen and give it a whirl. It's the best way I know to entertain the Goddess and get the help you need.

## Planning Perfect Spells and Rituals

Effective magic benefits from careful planning. It's helpful to make an outline before setting a spell in motion. That way, you can better focus on the subject matter and make changes while there's still time.

For your convenience, a magical worksheet has been provided for you, as well as a set of magical association charts for plants, stones, symbols, and Goddesses (Appendices I through IV). Use the worksheet (*Magical Work Outline,* page 211) to jot down any spell-related data and the appropriate associations. Write your spell or ritual using the Appendices as guides. You may want to photocopy the worksheet so that you always have the book copy as a blank original to use over and over again.

# Afterword

During the time it took to write this book, many changes occurred in my life. Some were happy, easygoing changes. Others turned my world upside down. There was a move. A surgery. The loss of several family members. There were job changes, schedule changes, and more interruptions than I can count on both hands. But through all the chaotic fluxing and flexing, one thing remained constant. There was always a reason to celebrate.

No matter the circumstances, reasons to celebrate are always with us. They just don't always come to us on a silver platter. Sometimes they like to hide in the cracks and crevices of life. We have to search them out, dig them up, and dust them off. But in patiently working toward their discovery, these little reasons become valuable to us. They become more precious, treasured, and cherished. They motivate us to go forward, reach toward our goals, and accomplish more than we ever dreamed.

When you feel like life is crumbling around you, and we all do at one time or another, take some time out and look for the celebratory aspects. Look long. Look hard. You might find it in the mew of a kitten, the kiss of a puppy, or the croak of a frog leaping across a pond. It might come in the form of sunshine, a winter's snow, or a rainbow after a stormy day. You might find it anywhere. But more than likely, you'll find it within yourself.

Remember that your very existence alone is an excellent reason to celebrate. You are one of a kind—a rare treasured jewel—and your value only increases with time. Everyone you touch, everything you touch, is indelibly marked with the magic of your signature. Your touch strengthens strands in the cosmic web, changes lives, and clears perspectives. It makes the world a better place to live. It provides a very good reason to celebrate.

You are woman. Do you know how important that is? You were born with the power to procreate the human race, to nurture it, and to keep it strong and healthy. You were born with a strength unlike any other. It's the strength that rules countries, amends laws, and crushes injustice. You have the power to make a difference. That's another good reason to celebrate.

You are Crone. You've finally found each of your personal aspects, drawn them out of hiding, and melded with them again. You are experienced. You are balanced. You are wise. You are the complete woman, a Goddess, empowered by the sacred blood you hold inside. This strengthens your voice, perfects your clarity, and motivates your every movement. It gives you a valuable place in the world—a place that only Crones can share. A place that's like no other. And that's the best reason of all to celebrate.

# Appendices

# ❖ Appendix 1

## Herbs, Plants, Flowers, and Their Magical Associations

| | Anger Mgmt. | Anxiety Mgmt. | Beauty | Courage | Depression Mgmt. | Divination | Dreams | Health / Healing | Liberation | Lust / Sex | Menopause | Mental Powers | Protection | Psychic Ability | Strength | Stress Mgmt. | Success | Victory | Wisdom | Wishes |
|---|---|---|---|---|---|---|---|---|---|---|---|---|---|---|---|---|---|---|---|---|
| African Violet | | | | | | | | | | | | | ◆ | | | | | | | |
| Agrimony | | | | | | | | | | | | | ◆ | | | | | | | |
| All Heal | | | | | | | | | | | | ◆ | | | | | | | | |
| Allspice | | | | | | | | ◆ | | ◆ | | | | | | | | | | |
| Almond | ◆ | | | | | | | | | | | | | | | | | | | |
| Aloe Vera | | | | | | | | | | | | | ◆ | | | | | | | |
| Alyssum | | | | | | | | | | | | | ◆ | | | | | | | |
| Angelica | | | | | | | | | | | | | ◆ | | | | | | | |
| Anise | | | | | | | ◆ | | | | | | ◆ | | | | | | | |
| Apple | | | | | | | | ◆ | | | | | | | | | | | | |
| Arrowroot | | | | | | | | | | | | | ◆ | | | | | | | |
| Asafoetida | | | | | | | | | | | | | ◆ | | | | | | | |
| Avocado | | | ◆ | | | | | | | | | | | | | | | | | |
| Balm of Gilead | | | | | | | | | | | | | ◆ | | | | | | | |
| Barley | | | | | | | | ◆ | | | | | | | | | | | | |
| Basil | | | | | | | | | | | | | ◆ | | | | | | | |
| Bay Leaf | | | | | | | | ◆ | | | | ◆ | ◆ | | ◆ | | | ◆ | | ◆ |
| Birch | | | | | | | | | | | | | | | | | | | | |
| Blackberry | | | | | | | | ◆ | | | | | | | | | | | | |
| Black Cohosh | | | | | | | | | | | ◆ | | | | | | | | | |
| Bladderwrack | | | | | | | | | | | | | ◆ | | | | | | | |
| Boneset | | | | | | | | | | | | | ◆ | | | | | | | |
| Borage | | | | ◆ | | | | | | | | | | | | | | | | |
| Bromeliad | | | | | | | | | | | | | ◆ | | | | | | | |
| Broom | | | | | | | | | | | | | ◆ | | | | | | | |
| Burdock | | | | | | | | | | | | | ◆ | | | | | | | |
| Cactus | | | | | | | | | | | | | ◆ | | | | | | | |
| Calamus | | | | | | | | | | | | | ◆ | | | | | | | |
| Calendula | | | | | | | | | | | | | | | | ◆ | | | | |
| Camphor | | | | | | ◆ | | | | | | | | | | | | | | |
| Caraway | | | | | | | | | | ◆ | | ◆ | ◆ | | | | | | | |
| Carnation | | | | | | | | | | | | | ◆ | | ◆ | | | | | |
| Carrot | | | | | | | | | | ◆ | | | | | | | | | | |
| Catnip | ◆ | | ◆ | | ◆ | | | | | | | | | | | | | | | |

202

| | Anger Mgmt. | Anxiety Mgmt. | Beauty | Courage | Depression Mgmt. | Divination | Dreams | Health / Healing | Liberation | Lust / Sex | Menopause | Mental Powers | Protection | Psychic Ability | Strength | Stress Mgmt. | Success | Victory | Wisdom | Wishes |
|---|---|---|---|---|---|---|---|---|---|---|---|---|---|---|---|---|---|---|---|---|
| Cattail | | | | | | | | | | ◆ | | | | | | | | | | |
| Cedar | | | | ◆ | | | | ◆ | | | | | ◆ | | | | | | | |
| Celandine | | | | ◆ | | | | | | | | | | | | | | | | |
| Celery Seed | | | | | | | | | | | | ◆ | | ◆ | | | | | | |
| Chamomile | ◆ | ◆ | | | | | ◆ | | | | | | | | | ◆ | | | | |
| Chicory | | | | | | | | ◆ | | | | | | | | | | | | |
| Chrysanthemum | | | | | | | | | | | | ◆ | | | | | | | | |
| Cinnamon | | | | | | | ◆ | | | ◆ | | ◆ | ◆ | ◆ | | | ◆ | | | |
| Cinquefoil | | | | | | ◆ | | | | ◆ | | | ◆ | | | | | | | |
| Citronella | | | | | | | | | | | | | | ◆ | | | | | | |
| Clover | | | | | | | | | | | | | ◆ | | | | ◆ | | | |
| Cloves | | | | | | | ◆ | | | ◆ | | | ◆ | | | | | | | |
| Columbine | | | | ◆ | | | | | | | | | | | | | | | | |
| Comfrey | | | | | | | | ◆ | | | | | | | | ◆ | | | | |
| Cumin | | | | | | | | | | | | | ◆ | | | | | | | |
| Curry | | | | | | | | | | | | | ◆ | | | | | | | |
| Cyclamen | | | | | | | | | | | | | ◆ | | | | | | | |
| Cypress | | | | | | | ◆ | | | | | | ◆ | | | | | | | |
| Daisy | | | | ◆ | | | | | | | | | | | | | | | | |
| Damiana | | | | | | | | | | ◆ | | | | | | | | | | |
| Dandelion | | | | | | ◆ | | | | | | | | | | | | | | ◆ |
| Datura | | | | | | | | | | | | | ◆ | | | | | | | |
| Deerstongue | | | | | | | | | | ◆ | | | | | | | | | | |
| Dill | | | | | | | | | | ◆ | | | ◆ | | | | | | | |
| Dogwood | | | | | | | | | | | | | ◆ | | | | | | | ◆ |
| Dragon's Blood | | | | | | | | | | | | | ◆ | | | | | | | |
| Elder | | | | | | | | ◆ | | | | | ◆ | | | | | | | |
| Elecampane | ◆ | | | | | | | | | | | | ◆ | ◆ | | | | | | |
| Eucalyptus | | | | | | | | ◆ | | | | | ◆ | | | | | | | |
| Eyebright | | | | | | | | | | | | | | ◆ | | | | | | |
| Fennel | | | | | | | | ◆ | | | | | ◆ | | | | | | | |
| Feverwort | | | | | | | | | | | | | ◆ | | | | | | | |
| Flax | | ◆ | | | | | | ◆ | | | | | ◆ | ◆ | | | | | | |
| Fleabane | | | | | | | | | | | | | ◆ | | | | | | | |

| | Anger Mgmt. | Anxiety Mgmt. | Beauty | Courage | Depression Mgmt. | Divination | Dreams | Health / Healing | Liberation | Lust / Sex | Menopause | Mental Powers | Protection | Psychic Ability | Strength | Stress Mgmt. | Success | Victory | Wisdom | Wishes |
|---|---|---|---|---|---|---|---|---|---|---|---|---|---|---|---|---|---|---|---|---|
| Forget-me-not | | | | | | | | | | | | ◆ | | | | | | | | |
| Foxglove | | | | | | | | | | ◆ | | | ◆ | | | | | | | |
| Frankincense | | | | | | | | | | | | ◆ | | | | | | | | |
| Galangal | | | | | | | | | | ◆ | | | ◆ | ◆ | | | | | | |
| Garlic | | | | | | | | ◆ | | | | | | | | | | | | |
| Geranium | | | | | | | | | | | | | ◆ | | | | | | | |
| Ginger | | | | | | | | | | | | | | | | | ◆ | | | |
| Ginkgo | | | | | | | | | | | | ◆ | | | | | | | | |
| Ginseng | | | ◆ | | | | | ◆ | | ◆ | | ◆ | | | | | | | | |
| Goldenrod | | | | | | ◆ | | | | | | | | | | | | | | |
| Golden Seal | | | | | | | | ◆ | | | | | | | | | | | | |
| Ground Ivy | | | | | | ◆ | | | | | | | | | | | | | | |
| Hawthorne | | | | | ◆ | | | | | | | | | | | | | | | |
| Hazel | | | | | | | | | | | | ◆ | | | | | | | ◆ | ◆ |
| Hazelnut | | | | | | ◆ | | | | | | | | | | | | | | |
| Heather | | | | | | | | | | | | | ◆ | | | | | | | |
| Heliotrope | | | | | | | ◆ | ◆ | | | | | | | | | | | | |
| Henbane | | | | | | ◆ | | | | | | | | | | | | | | |
| Hibiscus | | | | | | ◆ | | | | ◆ | | | | | | | | | | |
| High Joan | | | | | | | | | | | | | | | | | ◆ | ◆ | | |
| Holly | | | | | | | | | | | | | ◆ | | | | | | | |
| Honeysuckle | | | | | ◆ | | | | | | | | ◆ | ◆ | | | | | | |
| Hops | | | | | | | | ◆ | | | | | | | | ◆ | | | | |
| Horehound | | | | | | | | ◆ | | | | ◆ | ◆ | | | | | | | |
| Houseleek | | | | | | | | | | | | | ◆ | | | | | | | |
| Hyacinth | | | | | ◆ | | | | | | | | ◆ | | | | | | | |
| Hyssop | | | | | | | | | | | | | ◆ | | | | | | | |
| Ivy | | | | | | | | ◆ | | | | | ◆ | | | | | | | |
| Jasmine | | | | | | | ◆ | | | | | | | | | | | | | |
| Job's Tears | | | | | | | | | | | | | | | | | | | | ◆ |
| Juniper | | | | | | | | | | | | | ◆ | | | | | | | |
| Lady's Slipper | | | | | | | | | | | | | ◆ | | | | | | | |
| Larkspur | | | | | | | | | | | | | ◆ | | | | | | | |
| Lavender | ◆ | | | | | | | | ◆ | | ◆ | | ◆ | | | ◆ | | | | |

| | Anger Mgmt. | Anxiety Mgmt. | Beauty | Courage | Depression Mgmt. | Divination | Dreams | Health / Healing | Liberation | Lust / Sex | Menopause | Mental Powers | Protection | Psychic Ability | Strength | Stress Mgmt. | Success | Victory | Wisdom | Wishes |
|---|---|---|---|---|---|---|---|---|---|---|---|---|---|---|---|---|---|---|---|---|
| Lemon Balm | ◆ | | | | ◆ | | | ◆ | | | | | | | | | ◆ | | | |
| Lemon Grass | | | | | | | | | | | | | | ◆ | | | | | | |
| Life Everlasting | | | | | | | | ◆ | | | | | | | | | | | | |
| Lilac | | | | | | | | | | | | | ◆ | | | | | | | |
| Lily | | | | | | | | | | | | | ◆ | | | | | | | |
| Lily of the Valley | | | | ◆ | | | | | | | | ◆ | | | | | | | | |
| Linden | | | | | | | | | | | | | ◆ | | | | | | | |
| Lotus | | | | | | | | | | ◆ | | ◆ | ◆ | | | | | | | |
| Lucky Hand | | | | | | | | | | | | | ◆ | | | | | | | |
| Mace | | | | | | | | | | | | | | ◆ | | | | | | |
| Maidenhair Fern | | | ◆ | | | | | | | | | | | | | | | | | |
| Mallow | | | | | | | | | | | | | ◆ | | | | | | | |
| Mandrake | | | | | | | | | | | | | ◆ | | | | | | | |
| Marigold | | | | | | | | | | | | | ◆ | ◆ | | | | | | |
| Marjorum | | | | ◆ | | | | | | | | | | | | | | | | |
| Masterwort | | | | ◆ | | | | | | | | | | | | | | | | |
| Meadowsweet | | | | | | ◆ | | | | | | | | | | | | | | |
| Mimosa | | | | | | | ◆ | | | | | ◆ | | | | | | | | |
| Mint | ◆ | | | | | | ◆ | ◆ | | | | | | | | | | | | |
| Mistletoe | | | | | | | | | ◆ | ◆ | | | | | | | | | | |
| Moon Flower | | | | | | | | | ◆ | | | | | | | | | | | |
| Morning Glory | | | | ◆ | | | | | | | | | | | | | | | | |
| Mugwort | | | | | | ◆ | ◆ | ◆ | | | | | ◆ | ◆ | ◆ | | | | | |
| Mullein | | | ◆ | | | | | | | | | | ◆ | | | | | | | |
| Mulberry | | | | | | | | | | | | | ◆ | | ◆ | | | | | |
| Mustard | | | | | | | | | | | | | ◆ | | | | | | | |
| Myrrh | | | | | | | | ◆ | | | | | ◆ | | | | | | | |
| Nasturtium | | | | | | | | ◆ | | | | | | | | | | | | |
| Nettle | | | | | | | | | | | | | ◆ | | | | ◆ | | | |
| Nutmeg | | | | | | | | ◆ | | | | | | | | | | | | |
| Oak | | | | | | | | ◆ | | | | | ◆ | | | | | | | |
| Oats | | | | | | | | | | | | | | | | ◆ | | | | |
| Olive | | | | | | | | ◆ | | | | | ◆ | | | | | ◆ | | |
| Onion | | | | | | | | ◆ | | | | | ◆ | | | | | | | |

| | Anger Mgmt. | Anxiety Mgmt. | Beauty | Courage | Depression Mgmt. | Divination | Dreams | Health / Healing | Liberation | Lust / Sex | Menopause | Mental Powers | Protection | Psychic Ability | Strength | Stress Mgmt. | Success | Victory | Wisdom | Wishes |
|---|---|---|---|---|---|---|---|---|---|---|---|---|---|---|---|---|---|---|---|---|
| Orange | | | | | | | | | | | | | | | | | ◆ | | | |
| Pansey | | | | | | | | | | | | ◆ | | | | | | | | |
| Parsley | | | | | | | | | | ◆ | | | ◆ | | | | | | | |
| Passion Flower | ◆ | | | | | | | | | | | | | | | ◆ | | | | |
| Pennyroyal | | | | | | | | | | | | | ◆ | | ◆ | | | | | |
| Peony | | | | | | | | | | | | | ◆ | | | | | | | |
| Pepper | | | | | | | | | | | | | ◆ | | | | | | | |
| Peppermint | | | | | | | | ◆ | | ◆ | | | | ◆ | | | | | | |
| Perriwinkle | | | | | | | | | | | | ◆ | ◆ | | | | | | | |
| Persimmon | | | | | | | | ◆ | | | | | | | | | | | | |
| Pine | | | | | | | | ◆ | | | | | ◆ | | | | | | | |
| Plaintain | | | | | | | | ◆ | | | | | ◆ | | ◆ | | | | | |
| Pomegranate | | | | | | ◆ | | | | | | | | | | | | | | |
| Primrose | | | | | | | | | | | | | ◆ | | | | | | | |
| Quince | | | | | | | | | | | | | ◆ | | | | | | | |
| Radish | | | | | | | | | | | | | ◆ | | | | | | | |
| Raspberry | | | | | | | | | | | | | ◆ | | | | | | | |
| Rattlesnake Root | | | | | | | | | | | | | ◆ | | | | | | | |
| Rhubarb | | | | | | | | | | | | | ◆ | | | | | | | |
| Rose | ◆ | | ◆ | | | | ◆ | | | | | | ◆ | ◆ | | | | | | |
| Rosemary | | | ◆ | | | ◆ | ◆ | | | ◆ | | | | | | | | | | |
| Rowan | | | | | | | | ◆ | | | | | ◆ | ◆ | | | ◆ | | ◆ | |
| Rue | | | | | | | | ◆ | | | | ◆ | ◆ | | | | | | | |
| Saffron | | | | ◆ | | | | ◆ | | | | | | | | | | | | |
| Sage | | | | | | | | | | ◆ | | | ◆ | | | | | | ◆ | ◆ |
| Sandalwood | | | | | | | | ◆ | | | | ◆ | ◆ | | | | | | | |
| Sesame | | | | | | | | | | ◆ | | | | | | | | | | |
| Shepherd's Purse | | | | ◆ | | | | ◆ | | | | | | | | | | | | |
| Skullcap | | ◆ | | | | | | | | | | | | | | ◆ | | | | |
| Snapdragon | | | | | | | | | | | | | ◆ | | | | | | | |
| Southernwood | | | | | | | | | | | | | ◆ | | | | | | | |
| Spanish Moss | | | | | | | | | | | | | ◆ | | | | | | | |
| Spearmint | | | | | | | | | | | | ◆ | | | | | | | | |
| Spikenard | | | | | | | | | | | | ◆ | | | | | | | ◆ | |

| | Anger Mgmt. | Anxiety Mgmt. | Beauty | Courage | Depression Mgmt. | Divination | Dreams | Health / Healing | Liberation | Lust / Sex | Menopause | Mental Powers | Protection | Psychic Ability | Strength | Stress Mgmt. | Success | Victory | Wisdom | Wishes |
|---|---|---|---|---|---|---|---|---|---|---|---|---|---|---|---|---|---|---|---|---|
| St. John's Wort | | | | | | | | | | | | | ♦ | | ♦ | ♦ | | | | |
| Star Anise | | | | | | | | | | | | | | ♦ | | | | | | |
| Summer Savory | | | | | | | | | | | | ♦ | | | | | | | | |
| Sunflower | | | | | | | | | | | | | | | | | | | | ♦ |
| Sweet Gum (pod) | | | | | | | | | | | | | | | | | | | | |
| Sweetpea | | | | ♦ | | | | | | | | | | | | | | | | |
| Sweet Woodruff | | | | | | | | | | | | | ♦ | | | | | | | |
| Thistle | | | | | | | | ♦ | | | | | ♦ | | ♦ | | | | | |
| Thyme | | | | ♦ | | | | ♦ | | | | | | ♦ | | | | | | |
| Tonka Bean | | | | ♦ | | | | | | | | | | | | | | | | ♦ |
| Tulip | | | | | | | | | | | | | ♦ | | | | | | | |
| Uva Ursa | | | | | | | | | | | | | | ♦ | | | | | | |
| Valerian | | ♦ | | | | | ♦ | | | | | | ♦ | | | | | | | |
| Vanilla | | | | | | | | | | ♦ | | | | | | | | | | ♦ |
| Vervain | ♦ | | | | | | | ♦ | | | | | ♦ | | | | | | | ♦ |
| Violet | | | | | | | | ♦ | | ♦ | | | ♦ | | | | | | | ♦ |
| Walnut | | | | | | | | | | | | | | | | | | | | ♦ |
| Willow | | | | | | | | ♦ | | | | | ♦ | | | | | | | |
| Wintergreen | | | | | | | | ♦ | | | | | ♦ | | | | | | | |
| Witch Hazel | | ♦ | | | | | | | | | | | ♦ | | | | | | | |
| Wolfbane | | | | | | | | | | | | | ♦ | | | | | | | |
| Wood Betony | | | | | | | | | | | | | ♦ | | | | | | | |
| Wormwood | | | | | | | | | | | | | ♦ | ♦ | | | | | | |
| Yarrow | | | | ♦ | | | | | | | | | | ♦ | | | | | | |
| Yerba Santa | | | | | | | | ♦ | | | | | | | | | | | | |
| Yohimbe | | | | | | | | | | ♦ | | | | | | | | | | |
| Yucca | | | | | | | | | | | | | ♦ | | | | | | | |

# ❖ Appendix 2

## Stones and Their Magical Associations

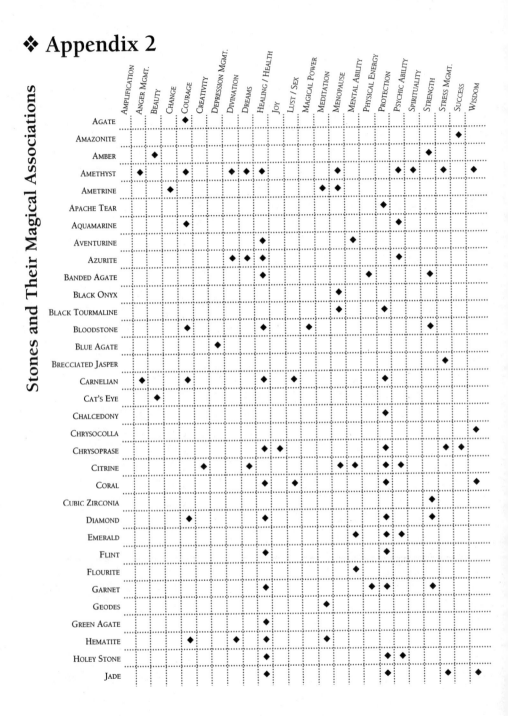

| | Amplification | Anger Mgmt. | Beauty | Change | Courage | Creativity | Depression Mgmt. | Divination | Dreams | Healing / Health | Joy | Lust / Sex | Magical Power | Meditation | Menopause | Mental Ability | Physical Energy | Protection | Psychic Ability | Spirituality | Strength | Stress Mgmt. | Success | Wisdom |
|---|---|---|---|---|---|---|---|---|---|---|---|---|---|---|---|---|---|---|---|---|---|---|---|---|
| Agate | | | | | ◆ | | | | | | | | | | | | | | | | | | | |
| Amazonite | | | | | | | | | | | | | | | | | | | | | | | ◆ | |
| Amber | | | ◆ | | | | | | | | | | | | | | | | | | | | | |
| Amethyst | ◆ | | | | ◆ | | | ◆ | ◆ | ◆ | | | | | ◆ | | | | ◆ | ◆ | ◆ | | | ◆ |
| Ametrine | | | | ◆ | | | | | | | | | | | ◆ | ◆ | | | | | | | | |
| Apache Tear | | | | | | | | | | | | | | | | | ◆ | | | | | | | |
| Aquamarine | | | | | ◆ | | | | | | | | | | | | | | | | | | | |
| Aventurine | | | | | | | | | | ◆ | | | | | | ◆ | | | | | | | | |
| Azurite | | | | | | | | ◆ | ◆ | ◆ | | | | | | | | | ◆ | | | | | |
| Banded Agate | | | | | | | | | | ◆ | | | | | | | | ◆ | | | ◆ | | | |
| Black Onyx | | | | | | | | | | | | | | | | ◆ | | | | | | | | |
| Black Tourmaline | | | | | | | | | | | | | | | | ◆ | | ◆ | | | | | | |
| Bloodstone | | | | | ◆ | | | | | ◆ | | | ◆ | | | | | | | | ◆ | | | |
| Blue Agate | | | | | | | | ◆ | | | | | | | | | | | | | | | | |
| Brecciated Jasper | | | | | | | | | | | | | | | | | | | | | ◆ | | | |
| Carnelian | ◆ | | | | ◆ | | | | | ◆ | | ◆ | | | | | | ◆ | | | | | | |
| Cat's Eye | | | ◆ | | | | | | | | | | | | | | | | | | | | | |
| Chalcedony | | | | | | | | | | | | | | | | | | | ◆ | | | | | |
| Chrysocolla | | | | | | | | | | | | | | | | | | | | | | | | ◆ |
| Chrysoprase | | | | | | | | | | | ◆ | ◆ | | | | | | | ◆ | | | | | |
| Citrine | | | | | | ◆ | | | | | ◆ | | | | ◆ | ◆ | | ◆ | ◆ | | | | | |
| Coral | | | | | | | | | | ◆ | | | ◆ | | | | | ◆ | | | | | | ◆ |
| Cubic Zirconia | | | | | | | | | | | | | | | | | | | ◆ | | | | | |
| Diamond | | | | | ◆ | | | | | ◆ | | | | | | | | ◆ | | | ◆ | | | |
| Emerald | | | | | | | | | | | | | | | | ◆ | | ◆ | ◆ | | | | | |
| Flint | | | | | | | | | | | | | | | | | ◆ | | | | | | | |
| Flourite | | | | | | | | | | | | | | | | | | ◆ | | | | | | |
| Garnet | | | | | | | | | | ◆ | | | | | | | | ◆ | ◆ | | ◆ | | | |
| Geodes | | | | | | | | | | | | | | ◆ | | | | | | | | | | |
| Green Agate | | | | | | | | | | ◆ | | | | | | | | | | | | | | |
| Hematite | | | | ◆ | | | | | | ◆ | | | | ◆ | | | | | | | | | | |
| Holey Stone | | | | | | | | | | ◆ | | | | | | | | | ◆ | ◆ | | | | |
| Jade | | | | | | | | | | ◆ | | | | | | | | | ◆ | | | | ◆ | ◆ |

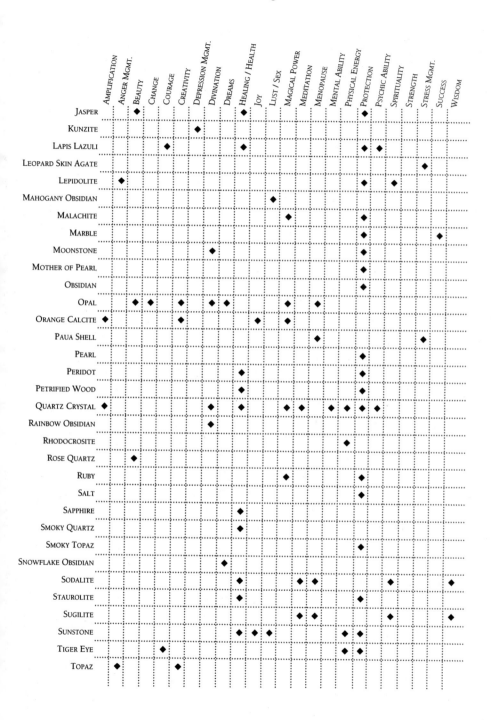

| | Amplification | Anger Mgmt. | Beauty | Change | Courage | Creativity | Depression Mgmt. | Divination | Dreams | Healing / Health | Joy | Lust / Sex | Magical Power | Meditation | Menopause | Mental Ability | Physical Energy | Protection | Psychic Ability | Spirituality | Strength | Stress Mgmt. | Success | Wisdom |
|---|---|---|---|---|---|---|---|---|---|---|---|---|---|---|---|---|---|---|---|---|---|---|---|---|
| Jasper | | | ◆ | | | | | | | ◆ | | | | | | | | ◆ | | | | | | |
| Kunzite | | | | | | | ◆ | | | | | | | | | | | | | | | | | |
| Lapis Lazuli | | | | ◆ | | | | | | ◆ | | | | | | | | ◆ | ◆ | | | | | |
| Leopard Skin Agate | | | | | | | | | | | | | | | | | | | | | | | ◆ | |
| Lepidolite | ◆ | | | | | | | | | | | | | | | | | ◆ | | ◆ | | | | |
| Mahogany Obsidian | | | | | | | | ◆ | | | | | | | | | | | | | | | | |
| Malachite | | | | | | | | | | | | ◆ | | | | | | ◆ | | | | | | |
| Marble | | | | | | | | | | | | | | | | | | ◆ | | | | | ◆ | |
| Moonstone | | | | | | | | ◆ | | | | | | | | | | ◆ | | | | | | |
| Mother of Pearl | | | | | | | | | | | | | | | | | | ◆ | | | | | | |
| Obsidian | | | | | | | | | | | | | | | | | | ◆ | | | | | | |
| Opal | | ◆ | ◆ | | | ◆ | | ◆ | ◆ | | | | ◆ | | ◆ | | | | | | | | | |
| Orange Calcite | ◆ | | | | | ◆ | | | | | ◆ | | ◆ | | | | | | | | | | | |
| Paua Shell | | | | | | | | | | | | | | ◆ | | | | | | | | | ◆ | |
| Pearl | | | | | | | | | | | | | | | | | | ◆ | | | | | | |
| Peridot | | | | | | | | | | ◆ | | | | | | | | ◆ | | | | | | |
| Petrified Wood | | | | | | | | | | ◆ | | | | | | | | ◆ | | | | | | |
| Quartz Crystal | ◆ | | | | | | | ◆ | | ◆ | | | ◆ | ◆ | | ◆ | ◆ | ◆ | ◆ | ◆ | | | | |
| Rainbow Obsidian | | | | | | | | | ◆ | | | | | | | | | | | | | | | |
| Rhodocrosite | | | | | | | | | | | | | | | | | | ◆ | | | | | | |
| Rose Quartz | | | ◆ | | | | | | | | | | | | | | | | | | | | | |
| Ruby | | | | | | | | | | | | | ◆ | | | | | ◆ | | | | | | |
| Salt | | | | | | | | | | | | | | | | | | ◆ | | | | | | |
| Sapphire | | | | | | | | | | ◆ | | | | | | | | | | | | | | |
| Smoky Quartz | | | | | | | | | | ◆ | | | | | | | | | | | | | | |
| Smoky Topaz | | | | | | | | | | | | | | | | | | ◆ | | | | | | |
| Snowflake Obsidian | | | | | | | | | ◆ | | | | | | | | | | | | | | | |
| Sodalite | | | | | | | | | | ◆ | | | | ◆ | ◆ | | | | | ◆ | | | | ◆ |
| Staurolite | | | | | | | | | | ◆ | | | | | | | | ◆ | | | | | | |
| Sugilite | | | | | | | | | | | | | | ◆ | ◆ | | | | | ◆ | | | | ◆ |
| Sunstone | | | | | | | | | | ◆ | ◆ | ◆ | | | | | ◆ | ◆ | | | | | | |
| Tiger Eye | | | | ◆ | | | | | | | | | | | | | ◆ | ◆ | | | | | | |
| Topaz | ◆ | | | | | ◆ | | | | | | | | | | | | | | | | | | |

| | Amplification | Anger Mgmt. | Beauty | Change | Courage | Creativity | Depression Mgmt. | Divination | Dreams | Healing / Health | Joy | Lust / Sex | Magical Power | Meditation | Menopause | Mental Ability | Physical Energy | Protection | Psychic Ability | Spirituality | Strength | Stress Mgmt. | Success | Wisdom |
|---|---|---|---|---|---|---|---|---|---|---|---|---|---|---|---|---|---|---|---|---|---|---|---|---|
| Turquoise | | | | | ◆ | | | | | ◆ | | | | | | | | ◆ | | | | | | |
| Unakite | | | ◆ | ◆ | | | | | | | ◆ | | | | | | | | | | | | | |
| Watermelon Tourmaline | | | | ◆ | ◆ | | | | | | | | | | | | | | | | | | | |
| Yellow Topaz | | | | | | | | | | ◆ | | | | | | | | | | | | | | |

# Magical Outline Worksheet

**Subject Matter:**

**Moon Phase:**

❑ WAXING ❑ FULL

❑ WANING ❑ DARK

**Corresponding Elements:**

❑ **AIR** ○ POSITIVE ○ NEGATIVE

❑ **FIRE** ○ POSITIVE ○ NEGATIVE

❑ **WATER** ○ POSITIVE ○ NEGATIVE

❑ **EARTH** ○ POSITIVE ○ NEGATIVE

**Deities:**

**Defining Your Tools:**

CANDLE COLOR: INCENSE:

HERBS:

STONES:

MAGICAL SYMBOLS:

**Chant / Invocation:**

# ❖ Appendix 3

**Magical Symbols for Feminine Empowerment**

| | Beauty | Change | Completion | Communication | Courage | Creativity | Dreams | Harmony | Healing / Health | Home | Joy | Justice | Knowledge | Liberation | Love / Romance | Lust / Sex | Magical Power | Menopause | New Endeavors | Obstacles |
|---|---|---|---|---|---|---|---|---|---|---|---|---|---|---|---|---|---|---|---|---|
| Acorn | | | | | ● | | | | | | | | | | | | | | ● | |
| Ankh | | | | | | | | | | | | | | | | | | ● | | |
| Apple | | | | | | | | | | | | | | | ● | | | | | |
| Armor | | | | | ● | | | | | | | | | | | | | | | |
| Arrow | | | | | ● | | | | | | | | | | | | | | | |
| Athame | | | | | | | | | | | | | | | | | ● | | | |
| Athletic Equipment | | | | | | | | | | | | | | | | | | | | |
| Bars | | | | | | | | | | | | | | | | | | | | ● |
| Bed | | | | | | ● | | | | | | | | | | ● | | | | |
| Bird | | | | | | | | | | | | | | ● | | | | | | |
| Bird's Nest | | | | | | | | | | | | | | | | | | | ● | |
| Blood | | | | | | | | | | | | | | | | | | | | |
| Blossoming Flower | | | | | | | | | | | | | | | | | | | | |
| Blue Star | | | | | | | | | | | | | | | | | | | | |
| Boat | | | | | | | | | | | | | | | | | | | | |
| Books | | | | | | | | | | | | ● | ● | | | | | | | |
| Budding Branch | | | | | | | | | | | | | | | | | | | ● | |
| Building Blocks | | | | | | | | | | | | | | | | | | | ● | |
| Bull | | | | | | | | | | | | | | | | | | | | |
| Business Suit | | | | | | | | | | | | | | | | | | | | |
| Butterfly | | ● | | | | | | | | | | | | ● | | | | ● | | |
| Candle Flame | | | | | | | | | | | | | ● | | | | | | | |
| Chalk | | | | | | ● | | | | | | | | | | | | | | |
| Circle | | ● | | | | | | | | | | | | | | | ● | | | |
| Closed Door | | | | | | | | | | | | | | | | | | | | ● |
| Closed Eyes | | | | | | | ● | | | | | | | | | | | | | |
| Cocoon | ● | | | | | | | | | | | | | | | | | | ● | |
| Computer | | | | ● | | | | | | | | | | | | | | | | |
| Computer Disk | | | | | | | | | | | | | ● | | | | | | | |
| Condom | | | | | | | | | | | | | | | | ● | | | | |
| Cornucopia | | | | | | | | | | | | | | | | | | | | |
| Crayons | | | | | | ● | | | | | | | | | | | | | | |
| Crown | | | | | | | | | | | | ● | | | | | | | | |
| Crystal | | | | | | | | | | | | | | | | | ● | | | |

| | Opportunity | Personal Growth | Physical Energy | Power | Prosperity | Protection | Psychic Ability | Strength | Stress Mgmt. | Success | Victory | Wisdom |
|---|---|---|---|---|---|---|---|---|---|---|---|---|
| Acorn | | | | | | | | | | | | |
| Ankh | | | | | | | | | | | | |
| Apple | | | | | | | | | | | | |
| Armor | | | | | | | | ◆ | | | | |
| Arrow | | | | ◆ | | | | | | | | |
| Athame | | | | | | | | | | | | |
| Athletic Equipment | | ◆ | | | | | | | | | | |
| Bars | | | | | | | | | | | | |
| Bed | | | | | | | | | | | | |
| Bird | | | | | | | | | | | | |
| Bird's Nest | | | | | | | | | | | | |
| Blood | | | | | | | | ◆ | | | | |
| Blossoming Flower | ◆ | | | | | | | | | | | |
| Blue Star | | | | | | ◆ | | | | | | |
| Boat | ◆ | | | | | | | | | | | |
| Books | | | | | | | | | | | | ◆ |
| Budding Branch | | | | | | | | | | | | |
| Building Blocks | | | | | | | | | | | | |
| Bull | | | | | | | | ◆ | | | | |
| Business Suit | | | | | | | | | | ◆ | | |
| Butterfly | | | | | | | | | | | | |
| Candle Flame | | | | | | | | | | | | |
| Chalk | | | | | | | | | | | | |
| Circle | | | | | | | | | | | | |
| Closed Door | | | | | | | | | | | | |
| Closed Eyes | | | | | | | | | | | | |
| Cocoon | | | | | | | | | | | | |
| Computer | | | | | | | | | | | | |
| Computer Disk | | | | | | | | | | | | |
| Condom | | | | | | | | | | | | |
| Cornucopia | | | | | ◆ | | | | | | | |
| Crayons | | | | | | | | | | | | |
| Crown | | | | | | | | | | | | |
| Crystal | | | | ◆ | | | ◆ | | | | | |

| | Beauty | Change | Completion | Communication | Courage | Creativity | Dreams | Harmony | Healing / Health | Home | Joy | Justice | Knowledge | Liberation | Love / Romance | Lust / Sex | Magical Power | Menopause | New Endeavors | Obstacles |
|---|---|---|---|---|---|---|---|---|---|---|---|---|---|---|---|---|---|---|---|---|
| Crystal Ball | | | | | | | | | | | | | | | | | | | | |
| Cup | | | | | | | | | | | | | | | | | | ✦ | | |
| Daisy | | | | | | | | | | | ✦ | | | | | | | | | |
| Diamond | | | | | | | | | | | | | | | | | | | | |
| Diploma | | | | | | | | | | | | | ✦ | | | | | | | |
| Dishes | | | | | | | | | | ✦ | | | | | | | | | | |
| Ear | | | | | | | | | | | | | | | | | | | | |
| Egg | | | | | | ✦ | | | | | | | | | | | | | ✦ | |
| Eye | | | | | | | | | | | | | | | | | | | | |
| Family Photo | | | | | | | | | | ✦ | | | | | | | | | | |
| Fence | | | | | | | | | | | | | | | | | | | | ✦ |
| Fire | | ✦ | | | | | | | | | | | | | | ✦ | | | | |
| Fireplace | | | | | | | | | | ✦ | | | | | | | | | | |
| Flower Bud | | | | | | | | | | | | | | | | | | | ✦ | |
| Full Moon Phase | | | | | | | | | | | | | | ✦ | | | | | | |
| Fur | | | | | | | | | | | | | | | | | | | | |
| Gavel | | | | | | | | | | | | ✦ | | | | | | | | |
| Hair | | | | | | | | | | | | | | | | | | | | |
| Hair Brush | ✦ | | | | | | | | | | | | | | | | | | | |
| Hands | | | | | | ✦ | | | | | | | | | | | | | | |
| Hat | | | | | | | | | | | | | | | | | | | | |
| Herb Bunches | | | | | | | | | ✦ | | | | | | | | | | | |
| House | | | | | | | | | | ✦ | | | | | | | | | | |
| Infinity Sign | | ✦ | | | | | | | | | | | ✦ | | | | ✦ | | | |
| Intertwined Hearts | | | | | | | | | | | | | | | ✦ | | | | | |
| Intertwined Rings | | | | | | | ✦ | | | | | | | | | | | | | |
| Jogging Suit | | | | | | | | | | | | | | | | | | | | |
| Keys | | | | | | | | | | | | | | ✦ | | | | | | |
| Knife | | | | | | | | | | | | | | ✦ | | | | | | |
| Laurel | | | | | | | | | | | | | | | | | | | | |
| Leaf | | | | | | | | | | | | | | | | | | | | |
| Light Bulb | | | | | | | | | | | | | ✦ | | | | | | | |
| Lightening Bolt | | ✦ | | | | | | | | | | | | | | | | ✦ | | |
| Lion | | | | | ✦ | | | | | | | | | | | | | | | |

| | Opportunity | Personal Growth | Physical Energy | Power | Prosperity | Protection | Psychic Ability | Strength | Stress Mgmt. | Success | Victory | Wisdom |
|---|---|---|---|---|---|---|---|---|---|---|---|---|
| Crystal Ball | | | | | | | ◆ | | | | | |
| Cup | | | | | | | | | | | | |
| Daisy | | | | | | | | | | | | |
| Diamond | | | | | ◆ | | | | | | | |
| Diploma | | | | | | | | | | | | |
| Dishes | | | | | | | | | | | | |
| Ear | | | | | | | ◆ | | | | | |
| Egg | ◆ | | | | | | | | | | | |
| Eye | | | | | | ◆ | ◆ | | | | | ◆ |
| Family Photo | | | | | | | | | | | | |
| Fence | | | | | | | | | | | | |
| Fire | | ◆ | | | | | | | | | | |
| Fireplace | | | | | | | | | | | | |
| Flower Bud | ◆ | | | | | | | | | | | |
| Full Moon Phase | | ◆ | | | ◆ | | | | | | | |
| Fur | | | | | ◆ | | | | | | | |
| Gavel | | | | | | | | | | | | |
| Hair | | | | ◆ | | | | | | | | |
| Hair Brush | | | | | | | | | | | | |
| Hands | | | | | | | | | | | | |
| Hat | | | | | | | | | | ◆ | | |
| Herb Bunches | | | | | | | | | | | | |
| House | | | | | | | | | | | | |
| Infinity Sign | | | | | | | | | | | | ◆ |
| Intertwined Hearts | | | | | | | | | | | | |
| Intertwined Rings | | | | | | | | | | | | |
| Jogging Suit | | | ◆ | | | | | | | | | |
| Keys | ◆ | | | | | | | | | | | |
| Knife | | | | | | | | | | | | |
| Laurel | | | | | | | | | | | ◆ | |
| Leaf | ◆ | | | | | | | | | | | |
| Light Bulb | | | | | | | | | | | | |
| Lightening Bolt | | | | | | | | | | | | |
| Lion | | | | | | | | ◆ | | | | |

| | Beauty | Change | Completion | Communication | Courage | Creativity | Dreams | Harmony | Healing / Health | Home | Joy | Justice | Knowledge | Liberation | Love / Romance | Lust / Sex | Magical Power | Menopause | New Endeavors | Obstacles |
|---|---|---|---|---|---|---|---|---|---|---|---|---|---|---|---|---|---|---|---|---|
| **Lipstick** | ◆ | | | | | | | | | | | | | | | | | | | |
| **Lock** | | | | | | | | | | | | | | | | | | | | ◆ |
| **Mailbox** | | | | ◆ | | | | | | | | | | | | | | | | |
| **Mars / Venus Signs** | | | | | | | | | | | | | | | | ◆ | | | | |
| **Medal** | | | | | | | | | | | | | | | | | | | | |
| **Mirror** | ◆ | | | | | | | | | | | | | | | | | | | |
| **Money** | | | | | | | | | | | | | | | | | | | | |
| **Moon Phases** | | ◆ | | | | | | | | | | | | | | | | | | |
| **Musical Note** | | | | | | ◆ | | ◆ | | | | | | | | | | | | |
| **Net** | | | | | | | | | | | | | | | | | | | | |
| **Newspaper** | | | | ◆ | | | | | | | | | | | | | | | | |
| **Open Door / Window** | | | | | | | | | | | | | | | | | | | | |
| **Owl** | | | | | | | | | | | | | | | | | | | | |
| **Paint / Brushes** | | | | | | | | | | | | | | | | | | | | |
| **Pajamas** | | | | | | | ◆ | | | | | | | | | | | | | |
| **Paper** | | | | | | | | | | | | | | | | | | | ◆ | |
| **Parrot** | | | | ◆ | | | | | | | | | | | | | | | | |
| **Pen / Pencil** | | | | ◆ | | ◆ | | | | | | | | | | | | | ◆ | |
| **Pentagram** | | | | | | | | | | | | | | | | | | | | |
| **Perfume Bottle** | ◆ | | | | | | | | | | | | | | | | | | | |
| **Pillow** | | | | | | | ◆ | | | | | | | | | | | | | |
| **Plants** | | | | | | | | | | | | | | | | | | | | |
| **Pomegranate** | | ◆ | | | | | | | | | | | | | | | | | | |
| **Rainbow** | | | | | | | | ◆ | | | | | | | | | | | | |
| **Raven** | | | | | | | | | | | | | | | | | | | | |
| **Rose** | | | | | | | | | | | | | | | ◆ | | | | | |
| **Satin Sheets** | | | | | | | | | | | | | | | | ◆ | | | | |
| **Scales** | | | | | | | | | | | | ◆ | | | | | | | | |
| **Scissors** | | | | | | | | | | | | | | ◆ | | | | | | |
| **Scroll** | | | ◆ | | | | | | | | | | | | | | | | | |
| **Severed Rope** | | | | | | | | | | | | | | ◆ | | | | | | |
| **Shield** | | | | | ◆ | | | | | | | | | | | | | | | |
| **Shoes** | | | | | | | | | | | | | | | | | | | ◆ | |
| **Smiley Face** | | | | | | | | | | | ◆ | | | | | | | | | |

| | Opportunity | Personal Growth | Physical Energy | Power | Prosperity | Protection | Psychic Ability | Strength | Stress Mgmt. | Success | Victory | Wisdom |
|---|---|---|---|---|---|---|---|---|---|---|---|---|
| Lipstick | | | | | | | | | | | | |
| Lock | | | | | | | | | | | | |
| Mailbox | | | | | | | | | | | | |
| Mars/Venus Signs | | | | | | | | | | | | |
| Medal | | | | | | | | | | | ◆ | |
| Mirror | | | | | | ◆ | | | | | | |
| Money | | | | | ◆ | | | | | ◆ | | |
| Moon Phases | | | | | | | | | | | | |
| Musical Note | | | | | | | | | ◆ | | | |
| Net | | | | | | | | ◆ | | | | |
| Newspaper | | | | | | | | | | | | |
| Open Door / Window | ◆ | | | | | | | | | | | |
| Owl | | | | | | | | | | | | ◆ |
| Paint / Brushes | | | | | | | | | | | | |
| Pajamas | | | | | | | | | | | | |
| Paper | | | | | | | | | | | | |
| Parrot | | | | | | | | | | | | |
| Pen / Pencil | | | | | | | | | | | | |
| Pentagram | | | | ◆ | | ◆ | | | | | | |
| Perfume Bottle | | | | | | | | | | | | |
| Pillow | | | | | | | | | ◆ | | | |
| Plants | | ◆ | | | | | | | | | | |
| Pomegranate | | | | | | | | | | | | |
| Rainbow | | | | | | | | | ◆ | | | |
| Raven | | | | | | | | | | | | ◆ |
| Rose | | | | | | | | | | | | |
| Satin Sheets | | | | | | | | | | | | |
| Scales | | | | | | | | | | | | |
| Scissors | | | | ◆ | | | | | | | | |
| Scroll | | | | | | | | | | | | |
| Severed Rope | | | | | | | | | | | | |
| Shield | | | | | | ◆ | | | | | | |
| Shoes | | | | | | | | | | | | |
| Smiley Face | | | | | | | | | ◆ | | | |

| | Beauty | Change | Completion | Communication | Courage | Creativity | Dreams | Harmony | Healing / Health | Home | Joy | Justice | Knowledge | Liberation | Love / Romance | Lust / Sex | Magical Power | Menopause | New Endeavors | Obstacles |
|---|---|---|---|---|---|---|---|---|---|---|---|---|---|---|---|---|---|---|---|---|
| Spider | | | | | | ◆ | | | | | | | | | | | | | | |
| Spider Web | | | | | | | | | | | | | | | | | | ◆ | | |
| Star | | | | | | | | | | | | | | | | | | | | |
| Steaming Teacup | | | | | | | | | ◆ | | | | | | | | | | | |
| Steaming Teapot | | ◆ | | | | | | | | | | | | | | | | | | |
| Sun | | | | | | | | | | | | | | | ◆ | | | | | |
| Sun / Moon | | | | | | | | | | | | | | | | | | | | |
| Sunflower | | | | | | | | | | | | | | | | | | | | |
| Sword | | | | | | | | | | | | | | | | | | | | |
| Tarot Cards | | | | | | | | | | | | | | | | | | | | |
| Telephone | | | | ◆ | | | | | | | | | | | | | | | | |
| Tennis Shoes | | | | | | | | | | | | | | | | | | | | |
| Triangle | | | | | | | | | | | | | | | | | | | | |
| Velvet | | | | | | | | | | | | | | | | | | | | |
| Vitamin Bottle | | | | | | | | | ◆ | | | | | | | | | | | |
| Wall | | | | | | | | | | | | | | | | | | | | ◆ |
| Wand | | | | | | | | | | | | | | | | | ◆ | | | |
| Waning Moon Phase | | | | | | | | | | | | | | | | | | ◆ | | |
| Waxing Moon Phase | | | | | | ◆ | | | | | | | | | | | | | | |
| Wedding Rings | | | | | | | | | | | | | | | ◆ | | | | | |
| Wine Glasses | | | | | | | | | | | | | | | ◆ | | | | | |
| Witch | | | | | | | | | | | | | | | | | ◆ | | | |
| Woman | ◆ | | | | | | | | | | | | | | | | | ◆ | | |
| Wreath | | | | | | | | | | | | | | | | | | | | |
| Yardstick | | | | | | | | | | | | | | | | | | | | |
| Your Name | | | | | | | | | | | | | | | | | | | | |

| | Opportunity | Personal Growth | Physical Energy | Power | Prosperity | Protection | Psychic Ability | Strength | Stress Mgmt. | Success | Victory | Wisdom |
|---|---|---|---|---|---|---|---|---|---|---|---|---|
| Spider | | | | | | | | | | | | |
| Spider Web | | | | | | ◆ | | | | | | ◆ |
| Star | | | | | | | | | | | ◆ | |
| Steaming Teacup | | | | | | | | | | | | |
| Steaming Teapot | | | | | | | | | | | | |
| Sun | ◆ | | | | ◆ | | | | ◆ | ◆ | | |
| Sun / Moon | | | | | | | | | | | | |
| Sunflower | | | | | | | | | | ◆ | | |
| Sword | | | ◆ | | | | | | | | | |
| Tarot Cards | | | | | | | ◆ | | | | | |
| Telephone | | | | | | | | | | | | |
| Tennis Shoes | | ◆ | | | | | | | | | | |
| Triangle | | | | | | | | | | | | ◆ |
| Velvet | | | | | ◆ | | | | | | | |
| Vitamin Bottle | | ◆ | | | | | | | | | | |
| Wall | | | | | | | | | | | | |
| Wand | | | | ◆ | | | ◆ | | | | | |
| Waning Moon Phase | | | | | | | | | | | | |
| Waxing Moon Phase | | | | | | | | | | | | |
| Wedding Rings | | | | | | | | | | | | |
| Wine Glasses | | | | | | | | | | | | |
| Witch | | | | | | | | | | | | |
| Woman | | | | | | | | | | | | |
| Wreath | | | | | | | | | | | ◆ | |
| Yardstick | ◆ | | | | | | | | | | | |
| Your Name | | | | ◆ | | | | | | | | |

# ❖ Appendix 4

**Goddess Associations for Menopause**

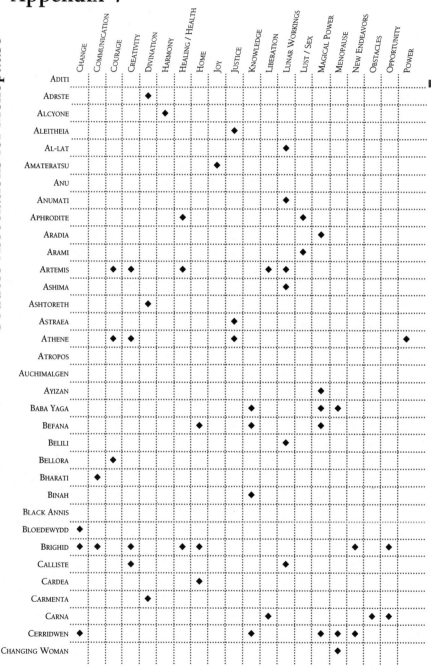

| | Change | Communication | Courage | Creativity | Divination | Harmony | Healing / Health | Home | Joy | Justice | Knowledge | Liberation | Lunar Workings | Lust / Sex | Magical Power | Menopause | New Endeavors | Obstacles | Opportunity | Power |
|---|---|---|---|---|---|---|---|---|---|---|---|---|---|---|---|---|---|---|---|---|
| ADITI | | | | | | | | | | | | | | | | | | | | |
| ADRSTE | | | | | ◆ | | | | | | | | | | | | | | | |
| ALCYONE | | | | | | ◆ | | | | | | | | | | | | | | |
| ALEITHEIA | | | | | | | | | | ◆ | | | | | | | | | | |
| AL-LAT | | | | | | | | | | | | | ◆ | | | | | | | |
| AMATERATSU | | | | | | | | | ◆ | | | | | | | | | | | |
| ANU | | | | | | | | | | | | | | | | | | | | |
| ANUMATI | | | | | | | | | | | | | ◆ | | | | | | | |
| APHRODITE | | | | | | | ◆ | | | | | | | | ◆ | | | | | |
| ARADIA | | | | | | | | | | | | | | | | ◆ | | | | |
| ARAMI | | | | | | | | | | | | | | | ◆ | | | | | |
| ARTEMIS | | | ◆ | ◆ | | | ◆ | | | | ◆ | | ◆ | | | | | | | |
| ASHIMA | | | | | | | | | | | | | ◆ | | | | | | | |
| ASHTORETH | | | | | ◆ | | | | | | | | | | | | | | | |
| ASTRAEA | | | | | | | | | | ◆ | | | | | | | | | | |
| ATHENE | | ◆ | ◆ | | | | | | | ◆ | | | | | | | | | | ◆ |
| ATROPOS | | | | | | | | | | | | | | | | | | | | |
| AUCHIMALGEN | | | | | | | | | | | | | | | | | | | | |
| AYIZAN | | | | | | | | | | | | | | | ◆ | | | | | |
| BABA YAGA | | | | | | | | | | | ◆ | | | | ◆ | ◆ | | | | |
| BEFANA | | | | | | | ◆ | | | | ◆ | | | | ◆ | | | | | |
| BELILI | | | | | | | | | | | | | ◆ | | | | | | | |
| BELLORA | | ◆ | | | | | | | | | | | | | | | | | | |
| BHARATI | ◆ | | | | | | | | | | | | | | | | | | | |
| BINAH | | | | | | | | | | | ◆ | | | | | | | | | |
| BLACK ANNIS | | | | | | | | | | | | | | | | | | | | |
| BLOEDEWYDD | ◆ | | | | | | | | | | | | | | | | | | | |
| BRIGHID | ◆ | ◆ | | ◆ | | | ◆ | ◆ | | | | | | | | | ◆ | | ◆ | |
| CALLISTE | | | | ◆ | | | | | | | | | ◆ | | | | | | | |
| CARDEA | | | | | | | ◆ | | | | | | | | | | | | | |
| CARMENTA | | | | ◆ | | | | | | | | | | | | | | | | |
| CARNA | | | | | | | | | | | ◆ | | | | | | | ◆ | ◆ | |
| CERRIDWEN | ◆ | | | | | | | | | | ◆ | | | | ◆ | ◆ | ◆ | | | |
| CHANGING WOMAN | | | | | | | | | | | | | | | | ◆ | | | | |

| | PROTECTION | PSYCHISM | STRENGTH | STRESS MGMT. | SUCCESS | VICTORY | WISDOM | WISHES |
|---|---|---|---|---|---|---|---|---|
| ADITI | ◆ | | | | | | | |
| ADRSTE | | | | | | | | |
| ALCYONE | | | | | | | | |
| ALEITHEIA | | | | | | | | |
| AL-LAT | | | | | | | | |
| AMATERATSU | | | | | | | | |
| ANU | | | | | ◆ | | | |
| ANUMATI | | | | | | | | |
| APHRODITE | | | | | | | | |
| ARADIA | | | | | | | | |
| ARAMI | | | | | | | | |
| ARTEMIS | | | ◆ | | | | | |
| ASHIMA | | | | | | | | |
| ASHTORETH | | | | | | | | |
| ASTRAEA | | | | | | | | |
| ATHENE | ◆ | | ◆ | | | | ◆ | |
| ATROPOS | | | | ◆ | | | | |
| AUCHIMALGEN | ◆ | | | | | | | |
| AYIZAN | | | | | | | | |
| BABA YAGA | | | | | | | | |
| BEFANA | | | | | | | | |
| BELILI | | | | | | | | |
| BELLORA | | | | | | | | |
| BHARATI | | | | | | | | |
| BINAH | | | | | | | | |
| BLACK ANNIS | ◆ | | | | | | | |
| BLOEDWYDD | | | | | | | | |
| BRIGHID | | | | | | | | |
| CALLISTE | | | | | | | | |
| CARDEA | | | | | | | | |
| CARMENTA | | | | | | | | |
| CARNA | | | | | | | | |
| CERRIDWYN | | | | | | | ◆ | ◆ |
| CHANGING WOMAN | | | | | | | | ◆ |

| | Change | Communication | Courage | Creativity | Divination | Harmony | Healing/Health | Home | Joy | Justice | Knowledge | Liberation | Lunar Workings | Lust/Sex | Magical Power | Menopause | New Endeavors | Obstacles | Opportunity | Power |
|---|---|---|---|---|---|---|---|---|---|---|---|---|---|---|---|---|---|---|---|---|
| CIRCE | | | | | | | | | | | | | | | ◆ | | | | | |
| CONCORDIA | | | | | | ◆ | | | | | | | | | | | | | | |
| DAKINIS | | | | | | | | | | | | | | | ◆ | | | | | |
| DEMETER | | | | | | | | | | | | | | | ◆ | | | | | |
| DESHTRI | | | | | | | | | | | ◆ | | | | | | | | | |
| DIANA | | ◆ | | | | | | | | | ◆ | ◆ | | | ◆ | | | | | |
| DIONE | | | | ◆ | | | | | | | | | | | | | | | | |
| DUGNAI | | | | | | | ◆ | | | | | | | | | | | | | |
| EDDA | | | | | | | | | | | ◆ | | | | | | | | | |
| EGERIA | | | | ◆ | | | | | | | | | | | | | | | | |
| EIR | | | | | | | ◆ | | | | | | | | | | | | | |
| EKADZATI | | | | | | | | | | | | | | | | | | | | |
| EPONA | ◆ | | | | | | | | | | | | | | | | | | | |
| ERIS | | | | | | | | | | | | | | | | | | | | |
| ERISHKEGAL | | | | | | | | | | | | | | | | | | | | |
| FILIA VOCIS | | | | ◆ | | | | | | | | | | | | | | | | |
| FORTUNA | | | | | | | | | | | | | | | | | | | | |
| FRIGGA | | | | | | | | | | | | | | | | | | | | |
| GAIA | | | | ◆ | | | | | | | | | | | | | | | | |
| GASMU | | | | | | | | | | | | | | | | | | | | |
| GULA | | | | | | | ◆ | | | | | | | | | | | | | |
| GULLEIG | | | | | | | | | | | | | | | ◆ | | | | | |
| GWENDYDD | | | | ◆ | | | | | | | | | | | | | | | | |
| HABONDI | | | | | | | | | | | | | | | ◆ | | | | | |
| HARMONIA | | | | | | ◆ | | | | | | | | | | | | | | |
| HATHOR | | | | | | | | | ◆ | | | | | ◆ | | | | | | |
| HECATE | | | | | | | | | | ◆ | ◆ | | | | ◆ | ◆ | | | | |
| HEKET | | | | | | | | | | | | | | ◆ | | | | | | |
| HERODIUS | | | | | | | | | | | | | | | ◆ | | | | | |
| HESTIA | | | | | | | | ◆ | | | | | | | | | | | | |
| HOLLE | | | | | | | | | | | | | | | ◆ | | | | | |
| HYGEIA | | | | | | | ◆ | | | | | | | | | | | | | |
| ILMATAR | | | ◆ | | | | | | | | | | | | | | | | | |
| INANNA | | | | ◆ | | | | | | | | | | | | | | | | |

| | PROTECTION | PSYCHISM | STRENGTH | STRESS MGMT. | SUCCESS | VICTORY | WISDOM | WISHES |
|---|---|---|---|---|---|---|---|---|
| CIRCE | | | | | | | | |
| CONCORDIA | | | | | | | | |
| DAKINIS | | | | | | | | |
| DEMETER | | | | | | | ◆ | |
| DESHTRI | | | | | | | | |
| DIANA | | ◆ | | ◆ | | | ◆ | |
| DIONE | | | | | | | | |
| DUGNAI | | | | | | | | |
| EDDA | | | | | | | | |
| EGERIA | | | | | | | | |
| EIR | | | | | | | | |
| EKADZATI | | | | | | | ◆ | |
| EPONA | | | | | | | | |
| ERIS | ◆ | | | | | | | |
| ERISHKEGAL | ◆ | | | | | | | |
| FILIA VOCIS | | | | | | | | |
| FORTUNA | | | | | ◆ | | | ◆ |
| FRIGGA | | | | | | ◆ | | |
| GAIA | | | | | | | | |
| GASMU | | | | | | | ◆ | |
| GULA | | | | | | | | |
| GULLEIG | | | | | | | | |
| GWENDYDD | | | | | | | | |
| HABONDI | | | | | | | | |
| HARMONIA | | | | | | | | |
| HATHOR | | | | | | | | |
| HECATE | ◆ | ◆ | | ◆ | | | ◆ | ◆ |
| HEKET | | | | | | | | |
| HERODIUS | | | | | | | | |
| HESTIA | | | | | | | | |
| HOLLE | | | | | | | | |
| HYGEIA | | | | | | | | |
| ILMATAR | | | | | | | | |
| INANNA | | | | | | | | |

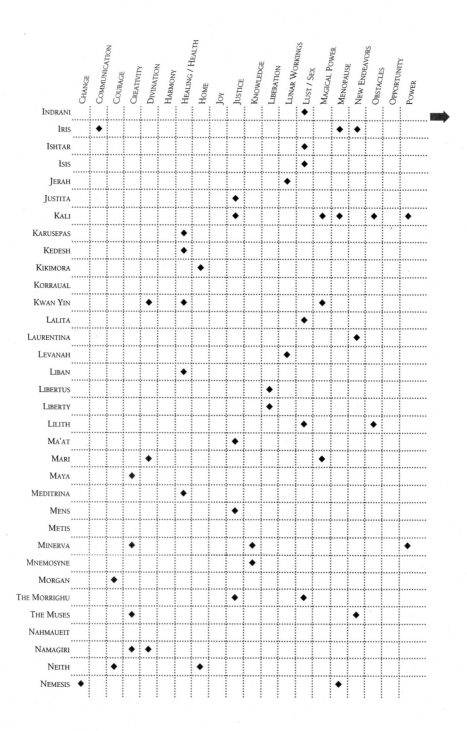

| | Change | Communication | Courage | Creativity | Divination | Harmony | Healing / Health | Home | Joy | Justice | Knowledge | Liberation | Lunar Workings | Lust / Sex | Magical Power | Menopause | New Endeavors | Obstacles | Opportunity | Power |
|---|---|---|---|---|---|---|---|---|---|---|---|---|---|---|---|---|---|---|---|---|
| INDRANI | | | | | | | | | | | | | | ♦ | | | | | | |
| IRIS | | ♦ | | | | | | | | | | | | | | ♦ | ♦ | | | |
| ISHTAR | | | | | | | | | | | | | | ♦ | | | | | | |
| ISIS | | | | | | | | | | | | | | ♦ | | | | | | |
| JERAH | | | | | | | | | | | | | ♦ | | | | | | | |
| JUSTITA | | | | | | | | | | ♦ | | | | | | | | | | |
| KALI | | | | | | | | | | ♦ | | | | | ♦ | ♦ | | ♦ | | ♦ |
| KARUSEPAS | | | | | | | ♦ | | | | | | | | | | | | | |
| KEDESH | | | | | | | ♦ | | | | | | | | | | | | | |
| KIKIMORA | | | | | | | | ♦ | | | | | | | | | | | | |
| KORRAUAL | | | | | | | | | | | | | | | | | | | | |
| KWAN YIN | | | | ♦ | | | ♦ | | | | | | | | ♦ | | | | | |
| LALITA | | | | | | | | | | | | | | ♦ | | | | | | |
| LAURENTINA | | | | | | | | | | | | | | | | | ♦ | | | |
| LEVANAH | | | | | | | | | | | | | ♦ | | | | | | | |
| LIBAN | | | | | | | ♦ | | | | | | | | | | | | | |
| LIBERTUS | | | | | | | | | | | | ♦ | | | | | | | | |
| LIBERTY | | | | | | | | | | | | ♦ | | | | | | | | |
| LILITH | | | | | | | | | | | | | | | ♦ | | | | ♦ | |
| MA'AT | | | | | | | | | | ♦ | | | | | | | | | | |
| MARI | | | | ♦ | | | | | | | | | | | ♦ | | | | | |
| MAYA | | | ♦ | | | | | | | | | | | | | | | | | |
| MEDITRINA | | | | | | | ♦ | | | | | | | | | | | | | |
| MENS | | | | | | | | | | ♦ | | | | | | | | | | |
| METIS | | | | | | | | | | | | | | | | | | | | |
| MINERVA | | | ♦ | | | | | | | ♦ | | | | | | | | | | ♦ |
| MNEMOSYNE | | | | | | | | | | | ♦ | | | | | | | | | |
| MORGAN | | ♦ | | | | | | | | | | | | | | | | | | |
| THE MORRIGHU | | | | | | | | | | ♦ | | | | | ♦ | | | | | |
| THE MUSES | | | ♦ | | | | | | | | | | | | | | ♦ | | | |
| NAHMAUEIT | | | | | | | | | | | | | | | | | | | | |
| NAMAGIRI | | | | ♦ | ♦ | | | | | | | | | | | | | | | |
| NEITH | | | ♦ | | | | ♦ | | | | | | | | | | | | | |
| NEMESIS | ♦ | | | | | | | | | | | | | | | ♦ | | | | |

| | Protection | Psychism | Strength | Stress Mgmt. | Success | Victory | Wisdom | Wishes |
|---|---|---|---|---|---|---|---|---|
| Indrani | | | | | | | | |
| Iris | | | | ◆ | | | | |
| Ishtar | | | | | | | | |
| Isis | | | | | | | | |
| Jerah | | | | | | | | |
| Justita | | | | | | | | |
| Kali | ◆ | | ◆ | | | | | |
| Karusepas | | | | | | | | |
| Kedesh | | | | | | | | |
| Kikimora | | | | | | | | |
| Korraual | | | | | | ◆ | | |
| Kwan Yin | | | | | | | | |
| Lalita | | | | | | | | |
| Laurentina | | | | | | | | |
| Levanah | | | | | | | | |
| Liban | | | | | | | | |
| Libertus | | | | | | | | |
| Liberty | | | | | | | | |
| Lilith | | | | | | | | |
| Ma'at | | | | | | | | |
| Mari | | | | | | | | |
| Maya | | | | | | | | |
| Meditrina | | | | | | | | |
| Mens | | | | | | | | |
| Metis | | | | | | | ◆ | |
| Minerva | | | | | | | ◆ | |
| Mnemosyne | | | | | | | | |
| Morgan | | | | | | | | |
| The Morrighu | | | | | | ◆ | | |
| The Muses | | | | | | | | |
| Nahmaueit | ◆ | | | | | | | |
| Namagiri | | | | | | | ◆ | |
| Neith | | | | | | | | |
| Nemesis | | | | | | | | |

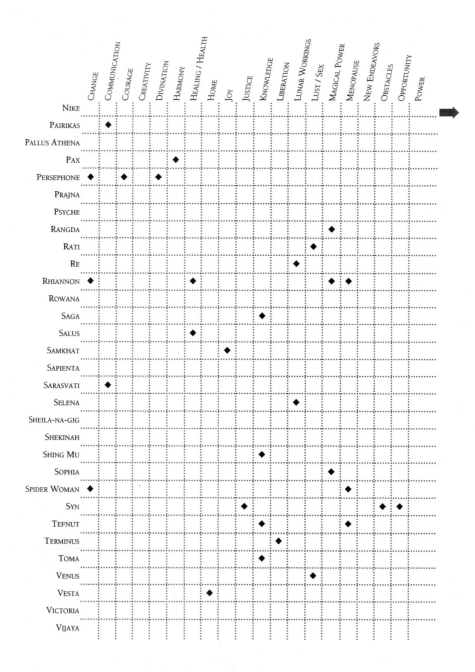

| | Change | Communication | Courage | Creativity | Divination | Harmony | Healing / Health | Home | Joy | Justice | Knowledge | Liberation | Lunar Workings | Lust / Sex | Magical Power | Menopause | New Endeavors | Obstacles | Opportunity | Power |
|---|---|---|---|---|---|---|---|---|---|---|---|---|---|---|---|---|---|---|---|---|
| Nike | | | | | | | | | | | | | | | | | | | | |
| Pairikas | | ♦ | | | | | | | | | | | | | | | | | | |
| Pallus Athena | | | | | | | | | | | | | | | | | | | | |
| Pax | | | | | | ♦ | | | | | | | | | | | | | | |
| Persephone | ♦ | | ♦ | | ♦ | | | | | | | | | | | | | | | |
| Prajna | | | | | | | | | | | | | | | | | | | | |
| Psyche | | | | | | | | | | | | | | | | | | | | |
| Rangda | | | | | | | | | | | | | | | ♦ | | | | | |
| Rati | | | | | | | | | | | | | | ♦ | | | | | | |
| Re | | | | | | | | | | | | | ♦ | | | | | | | |
| Rhiannon | ♦ | | | | | | ♦ | | | | | | | | ♦ | ♦ | | | | |
| Rowana | | | | | | | | | | | | | | | | | | | | |
| Saga | | | | | | | | | | | ♦ | | | | | | | | | |
| Salus | | | | | | | ♦ | | | | | | | | | | | | | |
| Samkhat | | | | | | | | | ♦ | | | | | | | | | | | |
| Sapienta | | | | | | | | | | | | | | | | | | | | |
| Sarasvati | | ♦ | | | | | | | | | | | | | | | | | | |
| Selena | | | | | | | | | | | | | ♦ | | | | | | | |
| Sheila-na-gig | | | | | | | | | | | | | | | | | | | | |
| Shekinah | | | | | | | | | | | | | | | | | | | | |
| Shing Mu | | | | | | | | | | | ♦ | | | | | | | | | |
| Sophia | | | | | | | | | | | | | | | ♦ | | | | | |
| Spider Woman | ♦ | | | | | | | | | | | | | | | ♦ | | | | |
| Syn | | | | | | | | | | ♦ | | | | | | | | | ♦ | ♦ |
| Tefnut | | | | | | | | | | | ♦ | | | | | ♦ | | | | |
| Terminus | | | | | | | | | | | | ♦ | | | | | | | | |
| Toma | | | | | | | | | | | ♦ | | | | | | | | | |
| Venus | | | | | | | | | | | | | | ♦ | | | | | | |
| Vesta | | | | | | | | ♦ | | | | | | | | | | | | |
| Victoria | | | | | | | | | | | | | | | | | | | | |
| Vijaya | | | | | | | | | | | | | | | | | | | | |

| | Protection | Psychism | Strength | Stress Mgmt. | Success | Victory | Wisdom | Wishes |
|---|---|---|---|---|---|---|---|---|
| Nike | | | | | | ◆ | | |
| Pairikas | | | | | | | | |
| Pallas Athena | | | | | | ◆ | | |
| Pax | | | | | | | | |
| Persephone | | | | | | | ◆ | |
| Prajna | | | | | | | ◆ | |
| Psyche | ◆ | | | | | | | |
| Rangda | | | | | | | | |
| Rati | | | | | | | | |
| Re | | | | | | | | |
| Rhiannon | | | | | | | | |
| Rowana | | ◆ | | | | | | |
| Saga | | | | | | | | |
| Salus | | | | | | | | |
| Samkhat | | | | | | | | |
| Sapienta | | | | | | | ◆ | |
| Sarasvati | | | | | | | | |
| Selena | | | | | | | | |
| Sheila-na-gig | ◆ | | | | | | | |
| Shekinah | | | | | | | ◆ | |
| Shing Mu | | | | | | | | |
| Sophia | | | | | | | ◆ | |
| Spider Woman | | | | | | | | |
| Syn | | | | | | | | ◆ |
| Tefnut | | | | | | | | |
| Terminus | | | | | | | | |
| Toma | | | | | | | | |
| Venus | | | | | | | | |
| Vesta | | | | | | | | |
| Victoria | | | | | | ◆ | ◆ | ◆ |
| Vijaya | | | | | | ◆ | | |

# Footnotes

To ensure your safety, the recipes in this book have been studied by licensed medicinal herbalists, alternative health care practitioners, and family practice physicians. They are deemed by all to be safe and healthy. Since every medical history is different, though, allowances must be made for extenuating circumstances. The following precaution and subsequent footnotes are therefore provided. You will note that some warnings refer to pregnancy and nursing. Though rare, post-menopausal pregnancies are not an impossibility. You can use this section as a general reference, but need only take into account what you and your health care practitioner deem applicable to your individual case.

> *Herbal Precaution.* If you are pregnant or nursing, take blood thinning agents, or suffer from hypertension, hypokalemia, edema, cirrhosis of the liver, cholastic liver disorders, or diabetes, please check with your personal health care practitioner before ingesting any of the following herbs: black cohosh, dong quai, licorice, motherwort.

1. *Motherwort*, page 89. See precaution above.
2. *Essential oils*, page 119. Keep oils out of reach of children. In case of ingestion, contact a poison control center immediately.

3. *Chamomile*, page 125. Chamomile is commonly enjoyed and entirely safe, but one should avoid using *Roman* chamomile during pregnancy.

4. *Sweet almond oil*, page 125. Do not substitute *bitter* almond oil during pregnancy.

5. *Dried comfrey*, page 125. For external use only. Do not use on broken or abraded skin for prolonged periods. Do not use during pregnancy.

6. *Dong quai*, page 165. See precaution above.

7. *Black cohosh*, page 165. See precaution above.

8. *Licorice*, page 165. Prolonged excessive use may cause hypertension, edema, headache, vertigo and potassium depletion. Moderate use, as outlined on page 165, is safe and healthy for everyone, though as per the precaution above, you should check with your health care giver if you have any of the conditions listed therein.

# Glossary

**ankh:** An Egyptian symbol of femininity. Constructed of an equal-armed cross with a circle on top, it is the astrological sign for Venus.

**asperge:** To sprinkle with a liquid, usually water. Asperging involves dipping a ritual tool of some type—a wand, athame, bunch of herbs, or a branch—into liquid, then shaking it off onto the item to be blessed or consecrated. Circles, spaces to be consecrated, or ritual items are often asperged as part of the cleansing or blessing ceremony.

**athame:** A consecrated double-edged knife—usually black-handled—used for Circle-casting, inscribing candles, and other ritual-related activities. According to most Pagan/Wiccan traditions, the athame must never be used to draw blood.

**deosil:** To move in a clockwise direction.

**dominant hand/arm:** This refers to the hand you use most often; i.e., for writing, to pick things up with, etc.

**magic:** The change of any condition through ritual means.

**pentagram:** An open-work, five-pointed star. The pentagram is a power symbol dating back to ancient times. Some practitioners call it the "macrocosm of man" because when we stand with our feet apart and our arms extended out from our sides, we form a human star. With one point up, the pentagram symbolizes the power of the mind (Akasha) over matter (the Elements). An inverted pentagram (two points up) represents matter over mind.

**third eye:** The point located just above the spot between the eyebrows. Many people call this area the "psychic center."

**Summerland:** A Pagan word for the place that the spirit resides in the afterlife. Some think of it as the Pagan equivalent to heaven.

**wand:** A ritual Circle-casting tool made of wood, metal, or stone. Traditionally, the wand is no larger in diameter than the practitioner's thumb, and is as long as the measurement between the bend of the elbow and the tip of the middle finger.

**widdershins:** To move in a counterclockwise direction.

# Bibliography

Ardinger, Barbara, Ph.D. *A Woman's Book of Rituals and Celebrations.* Novato, CA: New World Library, 1995.

Babcock, Michael. *The Goddess Paintings.* Rohnert Park, CA: Pomegranate Artbooks, 1994.

Beyerl, Paul. *Master Book of Herbalism.* Custer, WA: Phoenix Publishing, 1984.

Bremness, Lesley. *The Complete Book of Herbs: A Practical Guide to Growing and Using Herbs.* London: Dorling Kindersley Limited, 1988.

Brueton, Diana. *Many Moons; The Myth and Magic, Fact and Fantasy of our Nearest Heavenly Body.* New York: Prentice Hall Press, 1991.

Budapest, Zsuzsanna E. *The Goddess in the Office: A Personal Energy Guide for the Spiritual Warrior at Work.* New York: HarperCollins Publishers, 1993.

Cunningham, Scott. *Cunningham's Encyclopedia of Crystal, Gem and Metal Magic.* St. Paul, MN: Llewellyn Publications, 1987.

———. *Cunningham's Encyclopedia of Magical Herbs.* St. Paul, MN: Llewellyn Publications, 1986.

————. *The Complete Book of Oils, Incenses, and Brews.* St. Paul, MN: Llewellyn Publications, 1989.

David, Judithann H., Ph.D. *Michael's Gemstone Dictionary.* Channeled by J. P. Van Hulle. Orinda, CA: The Michael Educational Foundation and Affinity Press, 1986.

Dean, Carolyn, M.D. *Menopause Naturally.* New Canaan, CT: Keats Publishing, Inc., 1995.

Elias, Jason, and Katherine Ketcham. *In the House of the Moon: Reclaiming the Feminine Spirit of Healing.* New York: Warner Books, Inc., 1995.

Hamilton, Edith. *Mythology: Timeless Tales of Gods and Heroes.* New York: Mentor Books, 1940.

Hitchcock, Helyn. *Helping Yourself with Numerology.* West Nyack, NY: Parker Publishing Company, Inc., 1972.

Kerenyi, Karl. *Goddesses of Sun and Moon.* Translated from German by Murray Stein. Dallas, TX: Spring Publications, Inc., 1979.

Kunz, George Frederick. *The Curious Lore of Precious Stones.* Philadelphia, PA: J. B. Lippincott Company, © 1913; © 1941 by Ruby Kunz Zinsser; New York: Dover Publications, Inc., 1971, by special arrangement with J. P. Lippincott Company.

Malbrough, Ray T. *Charms, Spells & Formulas.* St. Paul, MN: Llewellyn Publications, 1986.

Medici, Marina. *Good Magic.* London: Macmillan London Limited, 1988; New York: Prentice Hall Press, 1989.

Melody. *Love is in the Earth: A Kaleidoscope of Crystals.* Wheat Ridge, CO: Earth-Love Publishing House, 1995.

Morrison, Sarah Lyddon. *The Modern Witch's Spellbook.* Secaucus, NJ: Citadel Press, 1971.

Nahmad, Claire. *Garden Spells.* Philadelphia, PA: Running Press Book Publishers, 1994.

Pepper, Elizabeth, and John Wilcock. *The Witches' Almanac: Spring 1994—Spring 1995*. Middletown, RI: Pentacle Press, 1994.

Rose, Jeanne. *Herbs and Things: Jeanne Rose's Herbal*. New York: Grosset & Dunlap/Workman Publishing Company, 1972.

Riva, Anna. *The Modern Herbal Spellbook: The Magical Uses of Herbs*. Toluca Lake, CA: International Imports, 1974.

Slater, Herman. *The Magickal Formulary*. New York: Magickal Childe Inc., 1981.

Starhawk. *The Spiral Dance: A Rebirth of the Ancient Religion of the Great Goddess*. New York: Harper & Row Publishers, Inc., 1979.

Tarostar. *The Witch's Spellcraft*. Toluca Lake, CA: International Imports, 1986.

Telesco, Patricia. *A Victorian Grimoire*. St. Paul, MN, Llewellyn Publications, 1992.

Walker, Barbara G. *The Woman's Encyclopedia of Myths and Secrets*. New York: Harper & Row Publishers, Inc., 1983.

Weed, Susun S. *Menopausal Years the Wise Woman Way*. Woodstock, NY: Ash Tree Publishing, 1992.

# Index

# ☽ REACH FOR THE MOON

*Llewellyn publishes hundreds of books on your favorite subjects! To get these exciting books, including the ones on the following pages, check your local bookstore or order them directly from Llewellyn.*

## ORDER BY PHONE

- Call toll-free within the U.S. and Canada, 1-800-THE MOON
- In Minnesota, call (612) 291-1970
- We accept VISA, MasterCard, and American Express

## ORDER BY MAIL

- Send the full price of your order (MN residents add 7% sales tax) in U.S. funds, plus postage & handling to:

  **Llewellyn Worldwide**
  **P.O. Box 64383, Dept. K368-9**
  **St. Paul, MN 55164–0383, U.S.A.**

## POSTAGE & HANDLING

(For the U.S., Canada, and Mexico)

- $4.00 for orders $15.00 and under
- $5.00 for orders over $15.00
- No charge for orders over $100.00

We ship UPS in the continental United States. We ship standard mail to P.O. boxes. Orders shipped to Alaska, Hawaii, The Virgin Islands, and Puerto Rico are sent first-class mail. Orders shipped to Canada and Mexico are sent surface mail.

**International orders:** Airmail—add freight equal to price of each book to the total price of order, plus $5.00 for each non-book item (audio tapes, etc.).

**Surface mail**—Add $1.00 per item.

*Allow 2 weeks for delivery on all orders.*
*Postage and handling rates subject to change.*

## DISCOUNTS

We offer a 20% discount to group leaders or agents. You must order a minimum of 5 copies of the same book to get our special quantity price.

**Visit our web site at www.llewellyn.com for more information.**

# Everyday Magic

*Dorothy Morrison*

Are you tired of looking for ritual solutions for today's problems: computer viruses, traffic that drives you crazy, and stress that makes you forget your own name? Does the quest for obscure spell ingredients leave you exhausted and empty-handed?

Now there's a better way to incorporate magic into your life without adding more stress to it. *Everyday Magic* updates the ancient arts to fit today's lifestyle. It promotes the use of modern convenience items as viable magical tools, and it incorporates the use of easy-to-find spell ingredients—most of which are already in your kitchen cabinet. It discusses the items and forces that boost magical work, as well as a multitude of time-saving tips and a large assortment of recipes for creating your own oils, incenses, potions, and powders. More than 300 spells and rituals cover the everyday concerns of the modern practitioner.

1-56718-469-3, 304 pp., 5 3/16 x 8, softcover        $9.95

# Magical
# Needlework

*Dorothy Morrison*

Creating beautiful and artistic handcrafts is in itself a magical act. Now, you can use your craft projects to further imbue your home with a magical atmosphere and evoke magical energy.

*Magical Needlework* explores the versatility of this magical art and offers a myriad of "hands-on" projects, ideas and patterns submitted by a wide spectrum of people within the spiritual community. You will discover the type of magical powers contains within various symbols, numbers, shapes, textures, stitches and weaves.

Sew a fairie dress for Midsummer Night's Eve and dancing in the moonlight . . . safeguard your home with an herbal protection charm . . . crochet a pentacle wallhanging . . . quilt an herbal soap bag and infuse it with magical success . . . knit a mediation mat for balance in your life . . . and much, much more.

1-56718-470-7, 224 pp., 8 1/2 x 11 7/8, photos, illus.      $17.95

**To order, call 1-800-THE-MOON**
Prices subject to change without notice

## The Complete Book of Incense, Oils & Brews

*Scott Cunningham*

For centuries the composition of incenses, the blending of oils, and the mixing of herbs have been used by people to create positive changes in their lives. With this book, the curtains of secrecy have been drawn back, providing you with practical, easy-to-understand information that will allow you to practice these methods of magical cookery.

Scott Cunningham, world-famous expert on magical herbalism, first published *The Magic of Incense, Oils and Brews* in 1986. *The Complete Book of Incense, Oils and Brews* is a revised and expanded version of that book. Scott took readers' suggestions from the first edition and added more than 100 new formulas. Every page has been clarified and rewritten, and new chapters have been added.

There is no special, costly equipment to buy, and ingredients are usually easy to find. The book includes detailed information on a wide variety of herbs, sources for purchasing ingredients, substitutions for hard-to-find herbs, a glossary, and a chapter on creating your own magical recipes.

**0-87542-128-8, 288 pp., 6 x 9, illus., softcover**             **$12.95**

# Mother Nature's Herbal

*Judith Griffin, Ph.D.*

A Zuni American Indian swallows the juice of goldenrod flowers to ease his sore throat . . . an East Indian housewife uses the hot spices of curry to destroy parasites . . . an early American settler rubs fresh strawberry juice on her teeth to remove tartar. People throughout the centuries have enjoyed a special relationship with Nature and her many gifts. Now, with *Mother Nature's Herbal*, you can discover how to use a planet full of medicinal and culinary herbs through more than 200 recipes and tonics. Explore the cuisine, beauty secrets and folk remedies of China, the Mediterranean, South America, India, Africa and North America. The book will also teach you the specific uses of flower essences, chakra balancing, aromatherapy, essential oils, companion planting, organic gardening and theme garden designs.

**1-56718-340-9, 7 x 10, 448 pp., 16-pg. color insert        $19.95**

### To order, call 1-800-THE-MOON
Prices subject to change without notice

## Earth, Air, Fire, & Water

*Scott Cunningham*

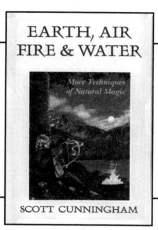

A water-smoothed stone . . . The wind . . . A candle's flame . . . A pool of water. These are the age-old tools of natural magic. Born of the Earth, possessing inner power, they await only our touch and intention to bring them to life.

The four Elements are the ancient powerhouses of magic. Using their energies, we can transform ourselves, our lives and our worlds. Tap into the marvelous powers of the natural world with these rites, spells and simple rituals that you can do easily and with a minimum of equipment. *Earth, Air, Fire & Water* includes more than 75 spells, rituals and ceremonies with detailed instructions for designing your own magical spells. This book instills a sense of wonder concerning our planet and our lives; and promotes a natural, positive practice that anyone can successfully perform.

**0-897542-131-8, 240 pp., 6 x 9, illus., softcover**　　　　**$9.95**

### To order, call 1-800-THE-MOON
Prices subject to change without notice